The

Berklee

Correspondence

Course

BERKLEE PRESS

Editor in Chief: Jonathan Feist
Senior Vice President of Online Learning and Continuing Education/CEO of Berklee Online: Debbie Cavalier
Vice President of Enrollment Marketing and Management: Mike King
Vice President of Academic Strategy: Carin Nuernberg
Editorial Assistant: Brittany McCorriston
Answer Key: Daniel Ian Smith

ISBN 978-1-54000-289-1

Berklee
Press

1140 Boylston Street
Boston, MA 02215-3693 USA
(617) 747-2146

Visit Berklee Press Online at
www.berkleepress.com

Berklee Online

Study music online at
online.berklee.edu

DISTRIBUTED BY

HAL•LEONARD®
7777 W. BLUEMOUND RD. P.O. BOX 13819
MILWAUKEE, WISCONSIN 53213

Visit Hal Leonard Online
www.halleonard.com

CONTENTS

INTRODUCTION

EDITOR'S NOTE

The Berklee Correspondence Course was first developed in the 1950s as a way to teach students at a distance—a precursor to today's Berklee Online. In those days, a student would receive lessons by mail and send their assignments back for grading by Berklee faculty.

This book is a reprinting of the 1971 edition. The content appears here essentially unchanged from that version, with the exception of some minor typographical practices that are more in keeping with our current house style. References to "contemporary style," "preferred practices," some terminology, and some strategies reflect what was favored at Berklee in the 1950s to the 1970s, which are not necessarily what we are currently teaching today.

An answer key to many of the activities is available online by accessing the code found on the first page of this book. Some require original composition, which of course will be unique for each reader. In these cases, samples reflecting correct practice are provided for your review.

We hope that you find this edition informative as a course in jazz composition and arranging, and interesting as a historical record of this innovative program, which helped launch the careers of so many musicians.

Jonathan Feist
Editor in Chief, Berklee Press
February, 2021

INTRODUCTION TO THE 1971 EDITION

You are about to embark on a course of study designed to give you, in the shortest possible time, a complete understanding of the principles of modern harmony, improvisation, and dance band arranging.

Naturally, the first lessons must be devoted to a discussion of the fundamentals of music, so that a common basic language may be established. You will find, however, that the work progresses quite rapidly, and that you will actually be scoring standard tunes as early as lesson 4, which deals with the four-part harmonization of a given melody.

Succeeding lessons will include:

- development of swing rhythms
- principles of improvisation
- theory of chord scales
- application of principles of improvisation
- modern four-part block harmonization
- use of tensions in improvisation
- chord progression
- substitute chords
- reharmonization
- etc., etc....

The actual lesson material, together with the comments and suggestions of your personal instructor, should combine to provide you with a comprehensive knowledge of the techniques of modern music and jazz, in practice as well as in principle.

Feel free to call upon your instructor for any further assistance or advice that you may require.

We are happy to be working with you, and wish you every success.

Correspondence Division
BERKLEE PRESS PUBLICATIONS

Elements of Music

Naturally, any study of music must begin with an understanding of those simple elements that go to make up music. The first of these elements to be discussed is pitch, which is designated by the location of a note on a musical stave. This is probably best explained by figure 1.1, which shows the location of each note in the "treble" and "bass" clefs.

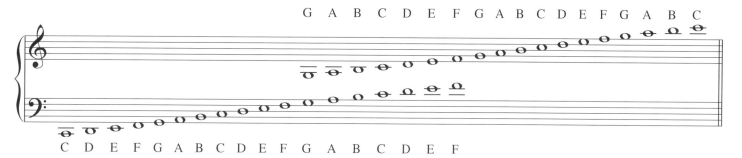

FIG. 1.1. Notes on Treble and Bass Clef

Some definitions relating to pitch:

semitone	The smallest distance between two notes.
whole tone	The equivalent of two semitones.
interval	The distance between two different pitches.
degree	Each note in a scale is called a "degree" of scale.
tetrachord	A four-note scale consisting of the following intervals: whole tone, whole tone, semitone.

The first direct application we will make of pitch is to the construction of major scales. A "scale" may best be defined as a series of related notes moving in a constantly ascending or descending direction.

MAJOR SCALE CONSTRUCTION

The *major scale* is made up of seven different notes, one on each successive line and space of the stave and each having a different letter name. The eighth note, or "octave," is added since this note gives a feeling of resolution and completion when the scale is played.

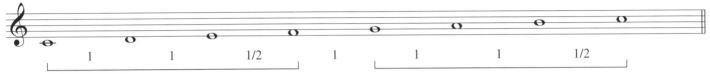

FIG. 1.2. Major Scale

Upon analyzing the intervals of the major scale built on C, you will find that the structure of the major scale is as follows: two tetrachords connected by a whole tone.

Whole tone, whole tone, semitone. (Tetrachord)
Whole tone.
Whole tone, whole tone, semitone. (Tetrachord)

These intervals between the degrees of the major scale never vary, hence, major scales may be built on any note using the structure of the scale built on C as a guide. A major scale built on the root tone A♭ would have the following appearance:

FIG. 1.3. Major Scale on A♭

Note that the fourth degree of this scale must be called D♭ rather than C♯, since the third degree had the letter name C, and the definition of a major scale stipulates that each of the scale degrees must fall on the next successive line or space and receive the next successive letter name. Just to be certain that the foregoing is perfectly clear, here is one more example of a major scale, this time built on the note E.

FIG. 1.4. Major Scale on E

Although major scales may be constructed as described above, a more organized method for finding all of the major scales and key signatures is based on the application of the tetrachord. As may be seen in the following example, the major scale is divisible into two equal parts, each part forming a tetrachord. These tetrachords are identical in construction and are connected by the interval of a whole tone.

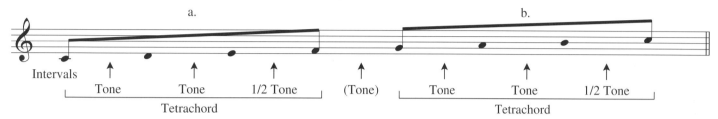

FIG. 1.5. Major Scale with Tetrachords

By using the *upper* tetrachord as the *lower* tetrachord in our new scale, it is possible to arrive at all of the key signatures containing sharps.

FIG. 1.6. Tetrachords on G

In figure 1.6, it is evident that the F must be sharped, since each tetrachord must be composed of whole tone, whole tone, half tone.

By following the same procedure, it is obvious that the next sharp key would begin with the tetrachord built on the note D—i.e., the upper tetrachord of the G scale.

FIG. 1.7. Tetrachords on D

Again, notice that the note C must be sharped in order to conform to the whole tone, whole tone, half tone structure of the tetrachord.

Beginning again with our C scale and this time using the lower tetrachord as the *upper* tetrachord of our new scale, it is possible to arrive at all of the key signatures containing flats.

FIG. 1.8. Tetrachords on F

Notice that in this case the B was flatted in order to conform to the tetrachord structure.

Once again, by using the lower tetrachord as the upper tetrachord of the new scale, it is evident that the next flat scale would have an upper tetrachord built on the note F and a new lower tetrachord constructed below it.

Lower Tetrachord of Previous Key (Fig. 1.8)   Giving Us the Key of B♭

FIG. 1.9. Tetrachords on B♭

Figure 1.10 shows the signatures of all of the sharp and flat keys in treble and bass clefs.

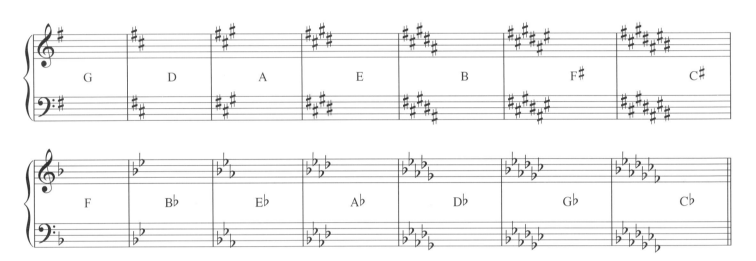

FIG. 1.10. All Key Signatures

NOTATION

There are certain basic principles to be followed in the correct and legible notation of music. Here are a few of them to help you in your work.

1. Make sure that every note is clearly centered on a line or a space.

FIG. 1.11. Bad vs. Good Note Placement

2. The same applies to the use of sharps and flats. If you are sharping the note F, be sure that the sharp is centered directly before the note.

FIG. 1.12. Bad vs. Good Accidental Placement

3. If a note has a stem attached to it, make sure that the stems are straight and try to observe the following rule: If the note is above the third line, stems go down; below the third line, stems go up.

FIG. 1.13. Stem Example

4. Always strive for a neat manuscript. It may take a little longer to complete the work at the start, but as you progress, you will develop speed together with a clear, legible manuscript.

(At this point it would be advisable to complete problems 1 through 6 of the assignment. See page 12.)

RHYTHM

Rhythm may be defined as the factor that controls duration—i.e., how long each note is to be held. Figure 1.14 shows each of the rhythmic values that will be used in succeeding lessons and the duration of time each occupies. The corresponding rests, shown on the right, represent the exact opposite: the absence of sound for a specified period of time.

	Name	Duration (When quarter note gets one beat)	Equivalent Rest
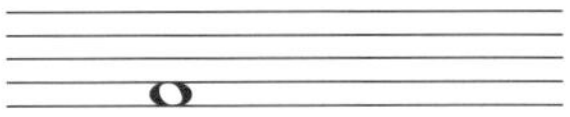	Whole Note	4 Beats	
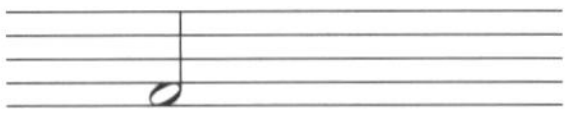	Half Note	2 Beats	
	Quarter Note	1 Beat	
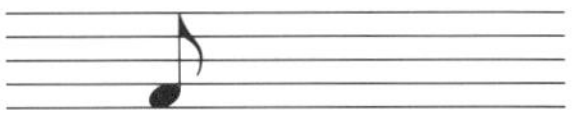	Eighth Note	1/2 Beat	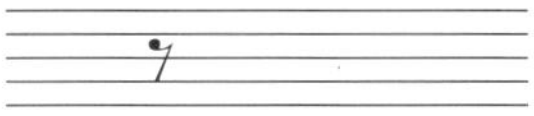
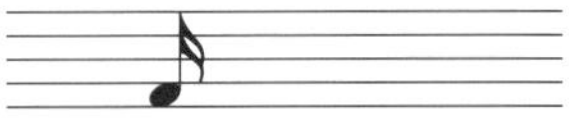	Sixteenth Note	1/4 Beat	
	Half-Note Triplet	4 Beats	
	Quarter-Note Triplet	2 Beats	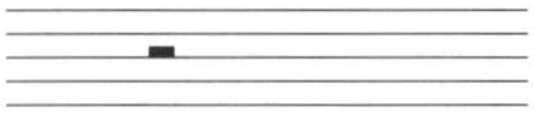
	Eighth-Note Triplet	1 Beat	
	Sixteenth-Note Triplet	1/2 Beat	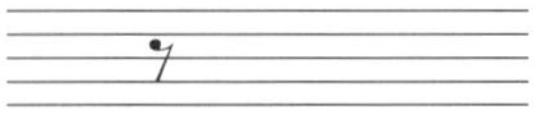
	Dotted Half Note	3 Beats	
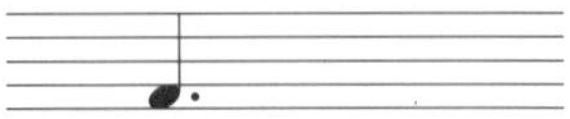	Dotted Quarter Note	1 1/2 Beats	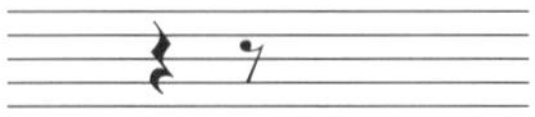

FIG. 1.14. Rhythmic Values

If the duration desired cannot be represented by any single note, it is achieved by combining two notes with a "tie." This means that the second note is not considered to be a new attack but is simply joined with the first as one duration.

FIG. 1.15. Tied Duration Example

The controlling factor in rhythm is the time signature. In each case the top number represents the number of beats or "counts" in a bar of music, while the bottom number tells us the kind of note that gets one beat.

4/4	6/8	2/2
4 beats per bar	6 beats per bar	2 beats per bar
quarter note gets 1 beat	eighth note gets 1 beat	half note gets 1 beat

FIG. 1.16. Time Signature Example

Assuming that a bar of 4/4 time can be written as four quarter notes, it is obvious that any combination of durations that add up to four will also form a bar of music in 4/4 time. Figure 1.17 presents several examples of measures in 4/4. Notice that each bar must contain some combination of durations that total four beats.

FIG. 1.17. Measures in 4/4

Next, some examples in 3/4 time:

FIG. 1.18. Measures in 3/4

The assignment work called for in this lesson should give you a good working knowledge of these simple rhythms, and an excellent foundation for understanding the syncopated and more complex rhythms to be discussed in future lessons.

CHORD CONSTRUCTION: TRIAD AND MAJOR 6

Using as a basis the major scales which are to be constructed as part of your lesson 1 assignment, it is possible to build all of the basic chords that are used in modern harmony and arranging.

The first of the basic chord structures that we will develop is the *major triad*, a three-part chord derived from the first, third, and fifth degrees of the major scale.

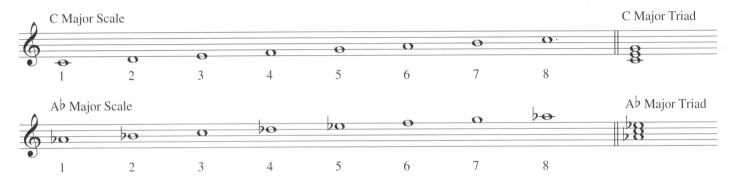

FIG. 1.19. Major Triads: C and A♭

However, since simple triads are rarely used in modern writing, we shall immediately move on to the more modern and fuller sounding version of major: the major 6 chord. The major 6 is a four-part chord derived from the first, third, fifth, and sixth degrees of the major scale.

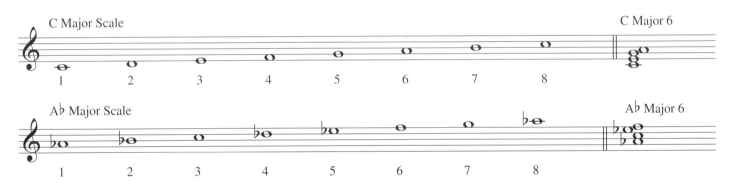

FIG. 1.20. Major 6 Chords: C6 and A♭6

As may be seen, the major and the major 6 are basically of the same tonality, and throughout this course, we will use the major 6 chord exclusively.

All types of chords are built from scales. At this time, however, it is important to learn and construct all of the major chords. This is accomplished through the development of "chord blocks," as shown on the next page.

SAMPLE PROBLEM

Fill in the open blocks.

6				Ⓒ
5			Ⓒ	
3		Ⓒ		
1	Ⓒ			
	b.	c.	d.	

FIG. 1.21. Fill-In Chord Block

The above exercise deals with major chords, hence the degrees 1, 3, 5, 6 are called for (see figure 1.20). The note C was selected arbitrarily.

1. First, fill in letter names without accidentals (sharps or flats).

   a. To fill in the blocks with C as 1 is a simple matter; merely count up alphabetically and use the letter names corresponding to the numbers called for.

   b. With C as 3, merely count down to 1 and up to 5 and 6.

   ⋯ G [A] B [C] D [E] [F] G A B ⋯
       1 2 3 4 5 6 7 8

   c. Similarly with C as 5, count down to 3 and 1 and up to 6.

   D E [F] G [A] B [C] [D] E F ⋯
        1 2 3 4 5 6 7 8

   d. Same treatment with C as 6.

   ⋯ B C D [E] F [G] A [B] [C] D ⋯
           1 2 3 4 5 6 7

The first step in the solution is now complete, and the chord block should appear as follows:

6	A	F	D	Ⓒ
5	G	E	Ⓒ	B
3	E	Ⓒ	A	G
1	Ⓒ	A	F	E

FIG. 1.22. Chord Block Solution

2. The second step is to check our major chord structures for necessary sharps or flats. *Do not alter the given note at any time.*

    a. With C as 1, we refer to that scale which has C as the first degree and find no sharps and no flats. Hence, 1, 3, 5, and 6 in this case are correct as they appear.

6	A			
5	G			
3	E			
1	Ⓒ			
	a.	**b.**	**c.**	**d.**

FIG. 1.23. Fill-In Chord Block: C

    b. With C as 3, refer to that scale that has C (natural) as the third degree. This we find to be the scale of A♭, which has a key signature of four flats (B♭, E♭, A♭, and D♭).

We must, therefore, correct the letter names to suit the scale. In this case A and E must be flatted.

6	A	F		
5	G	E♭		
3	E	Ⓒ		
1	Ⓒ	A♭		

FIG. 1.24. Fill-In Chord Block: A

3. With C as the fifth degree, we find that the appropriate scale is the scale of F with a signature of one flat (B♭). However, since there is no B called for in this chord, the other notes remain unaffected.

6	A	F	D	
5	G	E♭	Ⓒ	
3	E	Ⓒ	A	
1	Ⓒ	A♭	F	
	a.	b.	c.	

FIG. 1.25. Fill-In Chord Block: F

4.　With C as 6, we look for that scale which has the note C as the sixth degree. The proper scale in this case would be E♭ with a signature of three flats (B♭, E♭, A♭).

The notes that are affected in this case would be E and B, which must be flatted to conform to the scale.

6	A	F	D	Ⓒ
5	G	E♭	Ⓒ	B♭
3	E	Ⓒ	A	G
1	Ⓒ	A♭	F	E♭
	a.	b.	c.	d.

FIG. 1.26. Fill-In Chord Block: E♭ (Complete)

ASSIGNMENT

1.　(a)　Write five different examples of semitones.

　　(b)　Write five different examples of whole tones.

2.　Start with the scale of C, and through application of the tetrachord principle, work out all of the sharp key scales in both the treble and bass clefs.

3.　In the same manner, work out all of the flat key scales in both the treble and bass clefs.

4.　Complete the following problems as illustrated.

　　a.　C is the fifth note of the scale of F.

　　b.　F is the third note of the scale of _____.

　　c.　A♭ is the second note of the scale of _____.

　　d.　D is the seventh note of the scale of _____.

　　e.　F♯ is the sixth note of the scale of _____.

　　f.　E♭ is the fourth note of the scale of _____.

5.　Complete the following problems as illustrated.

　　a.　C is the third note of the scale of A♭ .

　　b.　F♯ is the _____ note of the scale of B.

　　c.　B is the _____ note of the scale of G.

　　d.　C♯ is the _____ note of the scale of E.

　　e.　D♭ is the _____ note of the scale of A♭.

　　f.　C is the _____ note of the scale of D♭.

6. Complete the following problems as illustrated.

   a. D is the third note of the scale of B♭.

   b. _____ is the seventh note of the scale of F.

   c. _____ is the fourth note of the scale of G♭.

   d. _____ is the seventh note of the scale of D.

   e. _____ is the sixth note of the scale of C♭.

   f. _____ is the third note of the scale of F♯.

7. Given are series of numbers. Write each of these series of duration in 4/4 time, as shown in figure 1.27.

FIG. 1.27. Durations in 4/4 Time

   a. 3, 1, 2, 3, 1, 3, 2, 1, 2, 3, 1, 2, 2, 1, 3, 2, 1, 2, 3, 1, 3, 2, 1, 3

   b. 2, 1, 3, 1, 5, 3, 1, 1, 2, 1, 4, 4, 1, 2, 1, 1, 3, 5, 1, 3, 1, 2

   c. ½, ½, 2, 2, 1, 5, ½, ½, 4, 2, ½, ½, ½, ½, 5, 1, 2, 2, 1, 3, ½, ½, ½, ½, 2, 4, ½, ½, 5

8. Write the same series of numbers, this time in 3/4 time.

FIG. 1.28. Durations in 3/4 Time

9. In this next problem dealing with rhythm, consider each of the circled numbers to indicate a corresponding period of rest.

   The rhythm: 1,(½,)½,(1,)½, 1½,(1½,)½, 1 would appear as follows in 4/4 time.

FIG. 1.29. Durations in 4/4 Time

Notate each of the following rhythmic phrases in 4/4 time.

   a. 2, 1,(1½,)1½,(1,)3,(1,)½, ½,(1,)4,(½,)½, 3,(1,)½, ½,(2,)1, 5,(1,)1, 1, 1½,(½,)1, 1, 3,(1,)½, ½, 1½,(1½,)2.

   b. (1,)1, 1, 1,(1½,)½, 5,(½,)½, ½, ½, 3, 2,(½,)½, 3, 1½, ½,(1,)1, 2, ½,(1½,)1, 2, (1,)1½,(1½,)1, 4,(½,)½, 1, 4.

   c. 3,(½,)½, 1, 1, 1, 1½,(1½,)2,(2,)1, 3,(1½,)½, 7, ½,(½,)2,(2,)1,(1,)1, ½, ½,(½,) ½, 1, 4,(1,)½, ½,(½,)1½, 2.

10. Again referring to the rhythmic patterns given in problem 9, notate each in 3/4 time.

11. Create a melody with a rhythm using notes of the E♭ major scale and a four-four time signature. This melody should be eight bars long and contain *scale* notes only.

Since the purpose of this assignment is to further your familiarization with the notes contained in the various keys, it is advisable that you use accidentals where needed, rather than a key signature.

Key of E♭

FIG. 1.30. Accidentals Instead of Key Signature

12. Write eight-bar melodies similar to that problem 11, but as follows:

Key of A: 4/4 time

Key of F: 4/4 time

Key of D♭:   4/4 time

Key of E: 3/4 time

Key of A♭:   4/4 time

Key of D: 3/4 time

Key of B♭:   4/4 time

Key of G: 3/4 time

13. Construct major chord blocks as described in this lesson on each of the following notes: C, F, B♭, E♭, B, E, A, D, G.

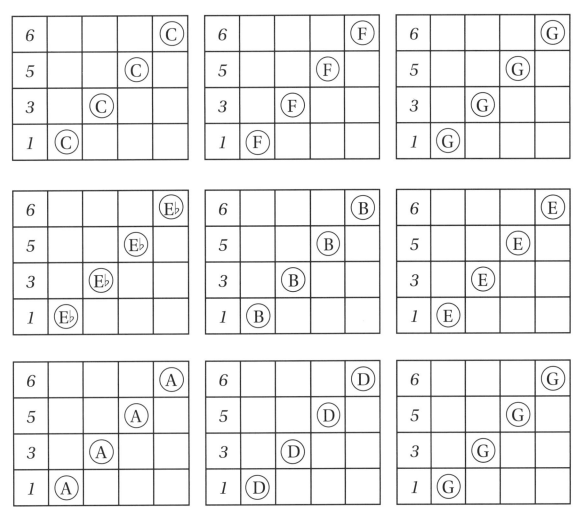

FIG. 1.31. Major 6 Chord Blocks

14. Write out each of the following major chords in musical notation with:

    a.   Root as bottom note

    b.   3 as bottom note

    c.   5 as bottom note

    d.   6 as bottom note

    on: C, D♭, D, E♭, E, F, F♯, G♭, G, A♭, A, B♭, B.

Inversions of the Major 6 Chord

FIG. 1.32. Inversions of the Major 6 Chord

15. The following problem is designed to familiarize you with major 6 chord structures. In composing the original melodies this time, use only *chord notes* of the major chord indicated above each bar.

FIG. 1.33. Sample Melody on Major 6 Chords

Compose original melodies on the following progressions using chord notes only.

FIG. 1.34. Write Your Own Melodies

Chord Construction and Voice Leading

CHORD CONSTRUCTION: MINOR TRIAD AND MINOR 6

To continue with our study of chords as begun in lesson 1, we shall now discuss and construct several more of the standard chord structures. The first of these is the *minor triad*. To construct the minor triad, simply refer to the major triad and lower the third degree one-half step.

FIG. 2.1. Major Triad to Minor Triad

In naming the lowered third degree, remember that if the original major third was sharped, the lowered third will be natural; if the major third was a natural, the lowered third will become a flat; and in the event that the major third was preceded by a flat, the lowered third will become a double flat (♭♭).

As explained in lesson 1, the simple triad is rarely used in modern chord voicing, so once again, we move on to the more commonly used minor chord with the added sixth. The *minor 6* chord may be found by referring to the major sixth and simply lowering the third degree one-half step.

FIG. 2.2. Major 6 to Minor 6

Once again, in order to properly construct and learn all of the minor 6 chords, it is advisable to make use of the "chord block" technique, as described in lesson 1. Here is a sample problem in constructing minor 6 chord blocks.

SAMPLE PROBLEM

Fill in the open blocks.

6				Ⓒ
5			Ⓒ	
Lowered 3		Ⓒ		
1	Ⓒ			
	a.	b.	c.	d.

FIG. 2.3. Minor 6 Chord Block on C

Figure 2.3 deals with minor chords, hence the degrees: 1, lowered 3, 5, and 6 are called for.

SOLUTION

1. First fill in letter names without accidentals with:

    a. C as the root

    b. C as the lowered 3

    c. C as the 5

    d. C as the 6

6	A	F	D	Ⓒ
5	G	E	Ⓒ	B
Lowered 3	E	Ⓒ	A	G
1	Ⓒ	A	F	E
	a.	b.	c.	d.

FIG. 2.4. Minor 6 Chord Block Complete

2. The second step is to check the minor chord structure for necessary sharps or flats.

   a. With C as the root, we refer to the scale built on C. Although there are no accidentals in the C scale, we still flat the note E since the minor-chord structure demands that the third degree must be lowered in relation to the scale.

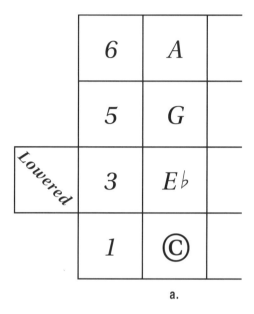

a.

FIG. 2.5. C Minor 6 with Accidental

   b. In this case, we must assume that the note C is already the lowered third degree of some scale. We know that in the scale of A major the C is sharped. Hence, the given C natural is correct as the lowered 3 in the scale of A. The sixth degree of A is F♯.

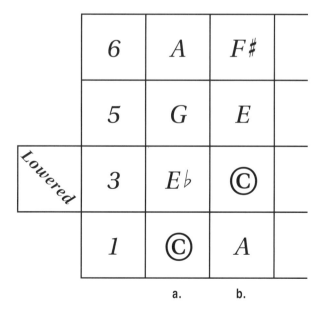

a.   b.

FIG. 2.6. A Minor 6 with Accidental

c. With C as the fifth degree, we refer to the scale of F. Again, all of the chord notes appear correct as they stand, but remembering that the third degree must be lowered to produce the minor chord, we find that the note A must be lowered to A♭.

		a.	b.	c.	
	6	A	F#	D	
	5	G	E	Ⓒ	
Lowered	3	E♭	Ⓒ	A♭	
	1	Ⓒ	A	F	

FIG. 2.7. F Minor 6 with Accidental

d. With C as the sixth degree, we refer to the scale of E♭. In addition to flatting the E and the B, we must lower the third degree to conform to the minor-chord structure, hence, G♭.

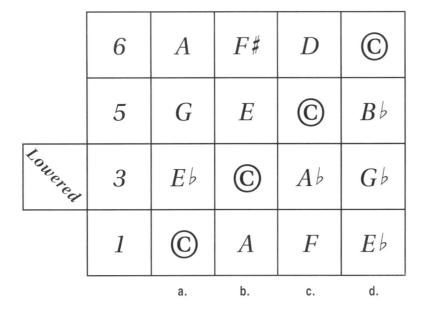

		a.	b.	c.	d.
	6	A	F#	D	Ⓒ
	5	G	E	Ⓒ	B♭
Lowered	3	E♭	Ⓒ	A♭	G♭
	1	Ⓒ	A	F	E♭

FIG. 2.8. Completed Minor C Chord Block with Accidentals (on C)

At this point, complete problems 1, 2, and 3 of assignment 2.

SEVENTH CHORDS: MAJOR AND DOMINANT

Another of the basic chords used in modern harmony is the *major seventh chord*. The major 7 is a four-part chord derived from the first, third, fifth, and seventh degrees of the major scale.

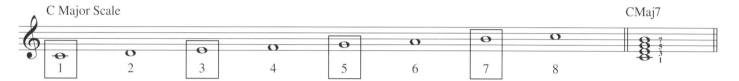

FIG. 2.9. C Major 7

Refer to problem 3 of assignment 2.

Since the major 7 is closely related to the major 6 chord, it will not be necessary to work out chord blocks on the major 7.

To continue with our study of the basic chord structures, we shall next consider the *dominant seventh chord*, a four-part chord, which is derived from the first, third, fifth and lowered seventh degrees of the major scale. The simplest method however, is to refer to the major seventh chord and lower the seventh degree one-half step.

FIG. 2.10. Major Seventh to Dominant Seventh

As in the case of the lowered third, if the original major seventh was a sharped note, we lower it by making it natural; if the original major seventh was a natural, the lowered seventh will become a flat; and in the event that the major seventh was already a flatted note, the lowered seventh would be double flatted (♭♭).

As we have already done with the major and minor chords, the chord block technique may once again be employed in constructing and learning all of the dominant seventh chords.

SAMPLE PROBLEM

Fill in the open blocks.

Lowered		a.	b.	c.	d.
	7				Ⓒ
	5			Ⓒ	
	3		Ⓒ		
	1	Ⓒ			

FIG. 2.11. Dominant 7 Chord Block on C

Since this exercise deals with dominant seventh chords, the degrees 1, 3, 5, and lowered seventh are called for.

SOLUTION

1. Fill in letter names without accidentals using:

   a. C as the root

   b. C as the 3

   c. C as the 5

   d. C as the lowered 7

Lowered		a.	b.	c.	d.
	7	B	G	E	Ⓒ
	5	G	E	Ⓒ	A
	3	E	Ⓒ	A	F
	1	Ⓒ	A	F	D

FIG. 2.12. Dominant 7 Chord Block Solution

2. Next, we check the dominant seventh chord structures for necessary sharps or flats.

a. With C as the root we refer to the C major scale. All of the notes are correct as they stand with the exception of the seventh degree B, which must be lowered to conform to the chord structure (dominant seventh).

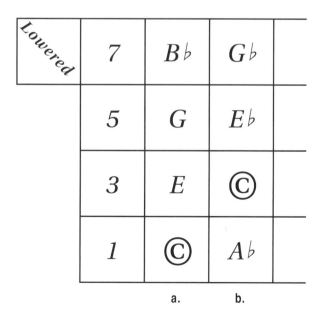

a.

FIG. 2.13. C Dominant 7 with Accidental

b. With C as the 3, the appropriate scale would be A♭, with a signature of four flats. In addition to flatting the A and the E to conform to the scale, the G must also be lowered to conform to the chord structure.

Lowered			
7	B♭	G♭	
5	G	E♭	
3	E	Ⓒ	
1	Ⓒ	A♭	
	a.	b.	

FIG. 2.14. A♭ Dominant 7 with Accidental

c. With C as the fifth degree of the F scale, the only alteration necessary would be to lower the seventh degree from E to E♭.

Lowered		a.	b.	c.
7		B♭	G♭	E♭
5		G	E♭	Ⓒ
3		E	Ⓒ	A
1		Ⓒ	A♭	F

FIG. 2.15. F Dominant 7 with Accidental

d. Here, we base our figuring on the fact that the note C is already the lowered seventh of some scale—in this case, the scale of D. We know that in the scale of D major, the C is sharped. Hence, the given C natural is correct as the lowered seventh in the scale of D. The third degree is F♯.

Lowered		a.	b.	c.	d.
7		B♭	G♭	E♭	Ⓒ
5		G	E♭	Ⓒ	A
3		E	Ⓒ	A	F♯
1		Ⓒ	A♭	F	D

FIG. 2.16. D Dominant 7 with Accidental

Before going on, it would be advisable to complete problems 4 and 5 of assignment 2.

NOTE: The following chord symbols are used in reference to the chord structures discussed in lessons 1 and 2.

C	C Major Sixth
Cmin	C Minor Sixth
CMaj7	C Major Seventh
C7	C Dominant Seventh

HARMONIC CONTINUITY

The first actual arranging technique that we will discuss is the principle of *harmonic continuity*, a method of producing smooth voice-leading in a given chord progression. Once you are completely familiar with this technique, it is a relatively simple matter to write interesting, effective backgrounds for any instrumental or vocal combination.

In these continuities, any chord may appear in any *inversion*, but no matter what the inversion, we shall name the notes in terms of voices rather than degrees. In other words, we shall consider the top note of the chord to be the first voice, the next note below it to be the second voice, and so forth.

FIG. 2.17. Inversions of C6

Once the position of the first chord is determined, to produce smooth voice leading to the following chord, simply apply the basic principle of harmonic continuity:

Keep the common tone (or tones) in the same voice (or voices).

To clarify this rule, let us assume that we are moving from a C chord to an A♭7 chord. We know that the notes of the C chord are C, E, G, A, and that the notes of the A♭7 chord would be A♭, C, E♭, G♭. In this case, the only common tone would be the note C, i.e., the only similar note found in both chords. In figure 2.18, C appears as the first voice of the C chord. Therefore, the C must remain as the first voice of the A♭7 chord, with the rest of the chord notes of the A♭7 being filled in below the C:

FIG. 2.18. Voice Leading from C (First Inversion) to A♭7

Were the C chord in the following position with the C as the second voice, then
the C would become the second voice of the A♭7 chord, and the following position
would result.

FIG. 2.19. Voice Leading from C (Second Inversion) to A♭7

In the event that the C chord were voiced so that the C was in the third or fourth
voice, the A♭7 would appear as follows:

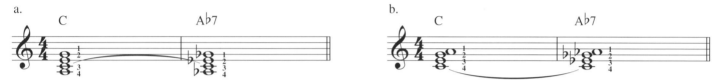

FIG. 2.20. Voice Leading from C (Third Inversion, then Root Position) to A♭7

To go on, let us assume that the A♭7 chord was followed by an Fmin chord. Now,
a common tone relationship must be established between the A♭7 chord and the
Fmin chord. The notes of the A♭7 chord are A♭, C, E♭, G♭; the notes of the Fmin
chord are F, A♭, C, D. In this case, there would be two common tones: A♭ and C (they
appear in both chords), and to produce smooth voice leading, they must be kept in
the same voices.

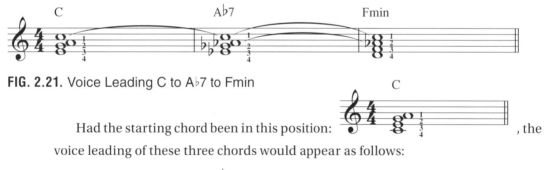

FIG. 2.21. Voice Leading C to A♭7 to Fmin

Had the starting chord been in this position: , the
voice leading of these three chords would appear as follows:

FIG. 2.22. Voice Leading C to A♭7 to Fmin: C in Root Position

Here is a longer example of a harmonic continuity with the common tones
indicated. The position of the starting chord was arbitrary.

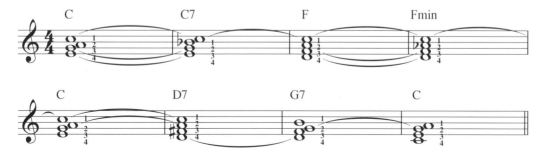

FIG. 2.23. Longer Voice-Leading Example

Occasionally, there will occur a situation where there are no common tones between adjacent chords. In this case, observe the following principle:

Where there are no common tones between adjacent chords, move the first voice to the nearest chord tone of the next chord (either above or below), and consider this to be the first voice of the new chord.

In the case of C to A♭min (no common tone), either of the following would be correct.

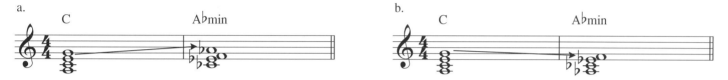

FIG. 2.24. C to A♭min Voice-Leading Examples

Here is a continuity incorporating this principle as well as the one previously discussed.

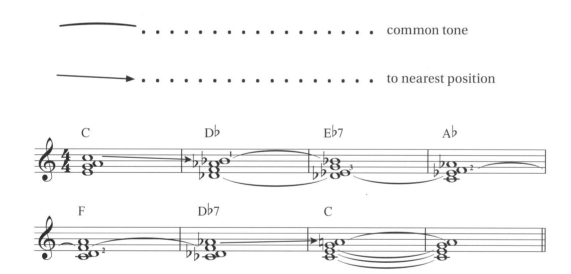

FIG. 2.25. Longer Voicing Example: Common Tones, Nearest Position

As you work out these harmonic continuities, you will notice that the progression has a tendency to move downward on the staff. This is a result of the natural downward tendency of most harmonic resolutions—one of the points that will be covered later in the course when we deal with the problems of setting up our own chord progressions or reharmonizing those that we are working with.

The following simple principle allows us to control the range of the continuity, a necessary device when we apply these chord patterns to orchestral writing.

As long as the chord remains the same, position may be freely changed without regard to voice leading.

As soon as the chord changes however, the common-tone principle must be observed.

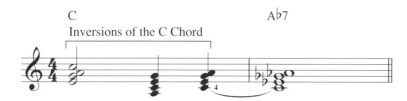

FIG. 2.26. Inversions of the C Chord

Now, to make sure that all of the foregoing is perfectly clear, here is a continuity containing all three of the principles applying to harmonic continuity.

inversion of the same chord

common tone

to nearest position

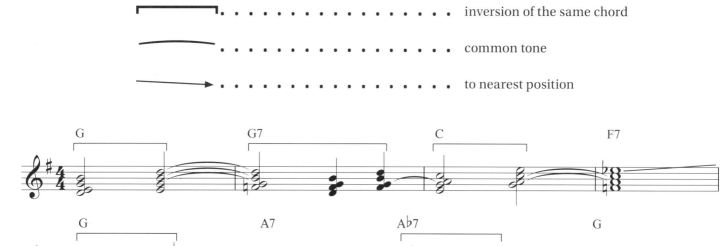

FIG. 2.27. Three Principles of Harmonic Continuity

ASSIGNMENT

1. Work out all minor sixth chord blocks indicated below.

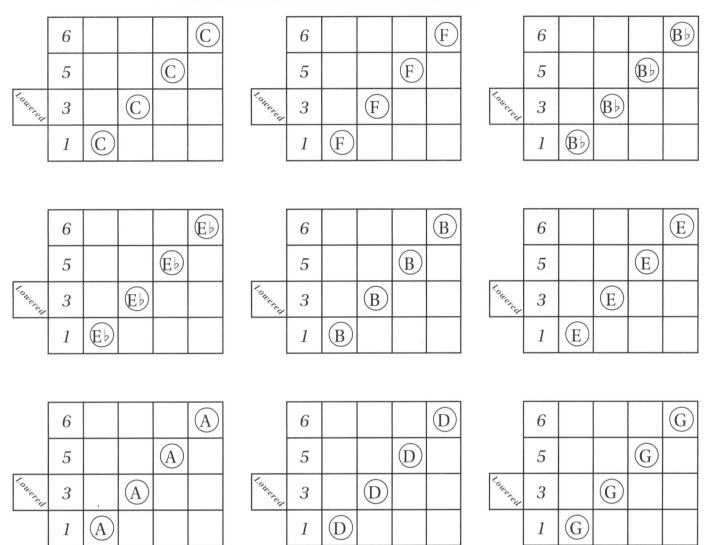

FIG. 2.28. Minor Chord Blocks

2. Notate minor 6 chords in all four inversions on each of the following notes:
   C, D♭, D, E♭, E, F, F♯, G♭, G, A♭, A, B♭, B.

FIG. 2.29. Inversions of the Minor Sixth Chord

3. Notate in all inversions, all major seventh chords (same list as in problem 2),

FIG. 2.30. Inversions of the Major Seventh Chord

4. Work out dominant 7 chord blocks as indicated below.

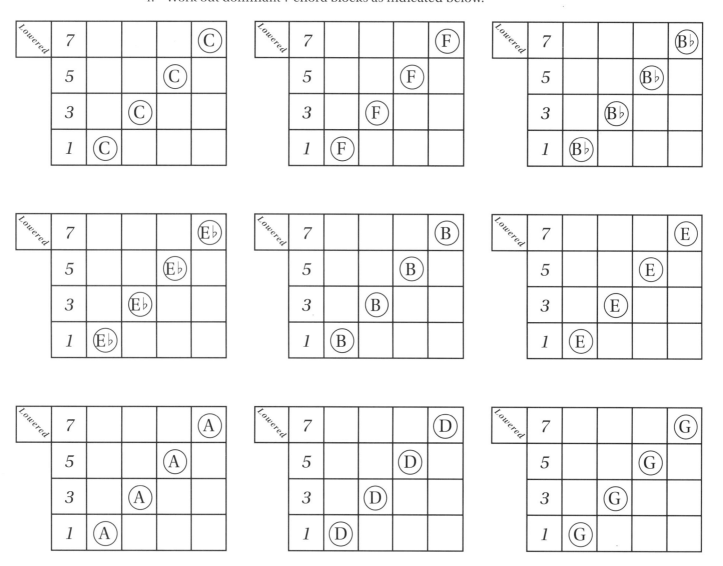

FIG. 2.31. Dominant 7 Chord Blocks

5. Notate inversions of the dominant 7 chord, again referring to the list of root tones given in problem 2.

FIG. 2.32. Inversions of the Dominant Seventh Chord

6. Write harmonic continuities on the following chord progressions. In working out these continuities, be sure to consider all of the principles covered in this lesson (see figure 2.27).

FIG. 2.33. Harmonic Continuity Practice

7. Set up a harmonic continuity plus an original melody on each of the following chord progressions using a three stave score as in the example below:

FIG. 2.34. Example Solution for Harmonic Continuity Practice

FIG. 2.35. Progressions for Harmonic Continuity Practice

Continuing Chord Construction

CHORD CONSTRUCTION: MINOR 7

To continue with our study of the basic chords, which are used in dance band work, we will next consider the *minor seventh chord*. The minor 7 is a four-part chord based on the root, lowered third, fifth, and lowered seventh of the major scale. A simple method that may be used to find the minor 7 would be to refer to the dominant 7 and lower the third degree one-half step.

a.

b.

FIG. 3.1. Dominant to Minor 7

Once again, in order to be certain that all of the minor 7 chords will be learned and constructed properly, we make use of the "chord block" technique as described in lessons 1 and 2.

SAMPLE PROBLEM

Fill in the open blocks.

		a.	b.	c.	d.
Lowered	7				Ⓒ
	5			Ⓒ	
Lowered	3		Ⓒ		
	1	Ⓒ			

FIG. 3.2. Fill-In Chord Block for Minor 7

Since we are dealing with the minor 7 chord, the degrees 1, lowered 3, 5, and lowered 7 are indicated.

SOLUTION

1. Determine letter names:

   a. with C as the root

   b. with C as the lowered 3

   c. with C as the 5

   d. with C as the lowered 7

Lowered	7	B	G	E	Ⓒ
	5	G	E	Ⓒ	A
Lowered	3	E	Ⓒ	A	F
	1	Ⓒ	A	F	D
		a.	b.	c.	d.

FIG. 3.3. Completed Minor 7 Chord Block on C

1. Add whatever sharps or flats may be needed to produce the minor 7 chord structure.

   a. With C as the root, we refer to the C major scale (no sharps or flats) and lower the third and seventh degrees (i.e., E and B) to conform to the chord structure.

Lowered	7	B♭
	5	G
Lowered	3	E♭
	1	Ⓒ
		a.

FIG. 3.4. C Minor 7 with Accidentals

b.   We find that C is the lowered 3 of the scale of A. (C♯ would be the regular
3.) We must also lower the 7: G♯ to G.

Lowered	7	B♭	G	
	5	G	E	
Lowered	3	E♭	Ⓒ	
	1	Ⓒ	A	
		a.	b.	

FIG. 3.5. A Minor 7 with Accidentals

c.   With C as the 5, we must refer to the scale of F. Again, to conform to the
minor 7 chord construction, we lower both the 3 and the 7.

Lowered	7	B♭	G	E♭
	5	G	E	Ⓒ
Lowered	3	E♭	Ⓒ	A♭
	1	Ⓒ	A	F
		a.	b.	c.

FIG. 3.6. F Minor 7 with Accidentals

d. With C as the lowered 7, the proper scale would be D major (regular seventh degree, C♯). In addition to the lowered 7, the 3 (F♯) must also be lowered to become F natural.

		a.	b.	c.	d.
Lowered	7	B♭	G	E♭	Ⓒ
	5	G	E	Ⓒ	A
Lowered	3	E♭	Ⓒ	A♭	F
	1	Ⓒ	A	F	D

FIG. 3.7. D Minor 7 with Accidentals

AUGMENTED

The next basic chord structure to be discussed is the *augmented triad*, a three-part chord based on the first, third, and raised fifth degrees of the major scale. A simple way to find the augmented triad would be to refer to the major triad and raise the fifth degree one-half step.

FIG. 3.8. Major to Augmented Triads

As stated previously, three-part chords are not often used in dance band arranging. The more commonly used form of this chord is the augmented seventh. In relation to the major scale, the augmented seventh chord would consist of the 1, 3, raised 5, and lowered 7. However, a simpler method would be to refer to the dominant 7 chord and raise the fifth degree one-half step.

FIG. 3.9. Dominant 7 to Augmented 7

It will not be necessary to work out chord blocks on the augmented seventh. If you are thoroughly familiar with all of the dominant 7 chord structures, you should have no difficulty in getting to know the augmented 7's.

DIMINISHED

Another of the chords with which you must be familiar is the *diminished triad*. The diminished triad is a three-part chord derived from the 1, lowered 3, and lowered 5 of the major scale. It may also be located by referring to the minor triad and simply lowering the fifth degree one-half step.

a.

b.

FIG. 3.10. Minor to Diminished Triad

Since we will need a four-part version of the chord for our arranging work, we move on to the *diminished 7 chord*, a four-part chord derived from the 1, lowered 3, lowered 5, and doubly lowered 7 of the major scale. Although it is called a seventh chord, the simplest method for building it would be to refer to the *minor sixth* chord and lower the fifth degree one-half step.

a.

b.

FIG. 3.11. Minor 6 to Diminished 7

Another feature of the diminished chord is that *enharmonic spelling* may be used freely without regard to scale degrees—i.e., F♯ may be called G♭; B♭♭ may be called A, etc. In figure 3.12, any of the chord spellings shown would be considered to be correct.

a.

b.

c.
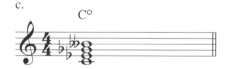

FIG. 3.12. Enharmonic Spellings of C Diminished 7

Again, as in the case of the augmented seventh chord, it will not be necessary to work out diminished seventh chord blocks. A thorough knowledge of the minor sixth chords should enable you to locate the diminished chord structure with little difficulty.

CHORD SYMBOLS

Every chord structure is designated by a special abbreviated name. Following is a complete listing of the basic chord structures that we will use, and the symbols that identify them.

STRUCTURE	SYMBOL
C Major	C
C Minor	Cmin, Cm, or C–
C Major 7	CMaj7
C Dominant 7	C7
C Minor 7	Cmin7, Cm7, or C–7
C Augumented 7	C Aug or C+
C Diminished 7	C dim or C°

FIG. 3.13. Basic Chord Structures and Symbols

In addition to these basic structures, you may occasionally encounter so-called "altered chords," where one of the regular chordal functions has been altered to produce a sound slightly different from that of the basic chord.

STRUCTURE	SYMBOL	NOTATION
D minor 7, lowered 5	Dmin7♭5	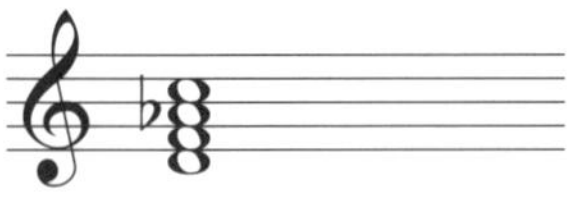

FIG. 3.14. Altered Chord Symbol and Notation

OPEN HARMONY

All of the chord positions that we have covered thus far belong to a general classification known as closed harmony. In addition to these closed voicings, certain open voicings may often be effectively used. A simple method for converting any chord from closed to open position may be described as follows:

> *To produce open harmony, drop the second voice (from the top) of any closed chord down one octave.*

To illustrate this principle, let us assume that we have a C major in the following closed position.

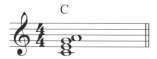

FIG. 3.15. C Major in Closed Position

To convert this chord from closed to open position, we would simply drop the second voice, G, down one octave.

FIG. 3.16. C Major in Open Position

If the closed C major chord had been voiced with the note E on top, dropping the second voice would result in the following open version of the C major chord.

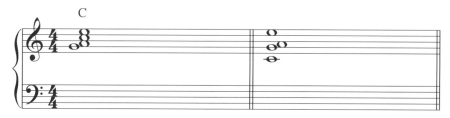

FIG. 3.17. C Major Closed and Open

Here are several more illustrations of open chords formed by dropping the second voice of closed chords.

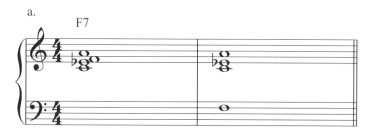

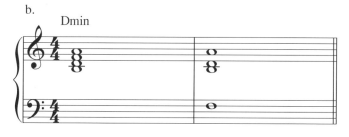

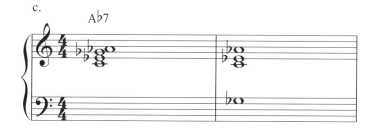

FIG. 3.18. Open Chord Examples

NOTE: When using open harmony, we may distribute the chord notes between the treble and the bass clefs, using the bass clef wherever the notes become so low that it would be inconvenient to write them in the treble clef. It is not necessary to keep a specified number of notes in each clef. Rather, use the bass clef where convenient to avoid the necessity of drawing ledger lines.

FIG. 3.19. Open Chords Using Bass Clef

It is of course possible (and quite effective musically) to apply the principle of open harmony to a harmonic continuity (see lesson 2). Here is an example of a continuity:

    a.   In closed position

    b.   Converted to open position by dropping the second voice down one octave

FIG. 3.20. Open Harmony Harmonic Continuity

ASSIGNMENT

1. Work out minor 7 chord blocks as indicated below.

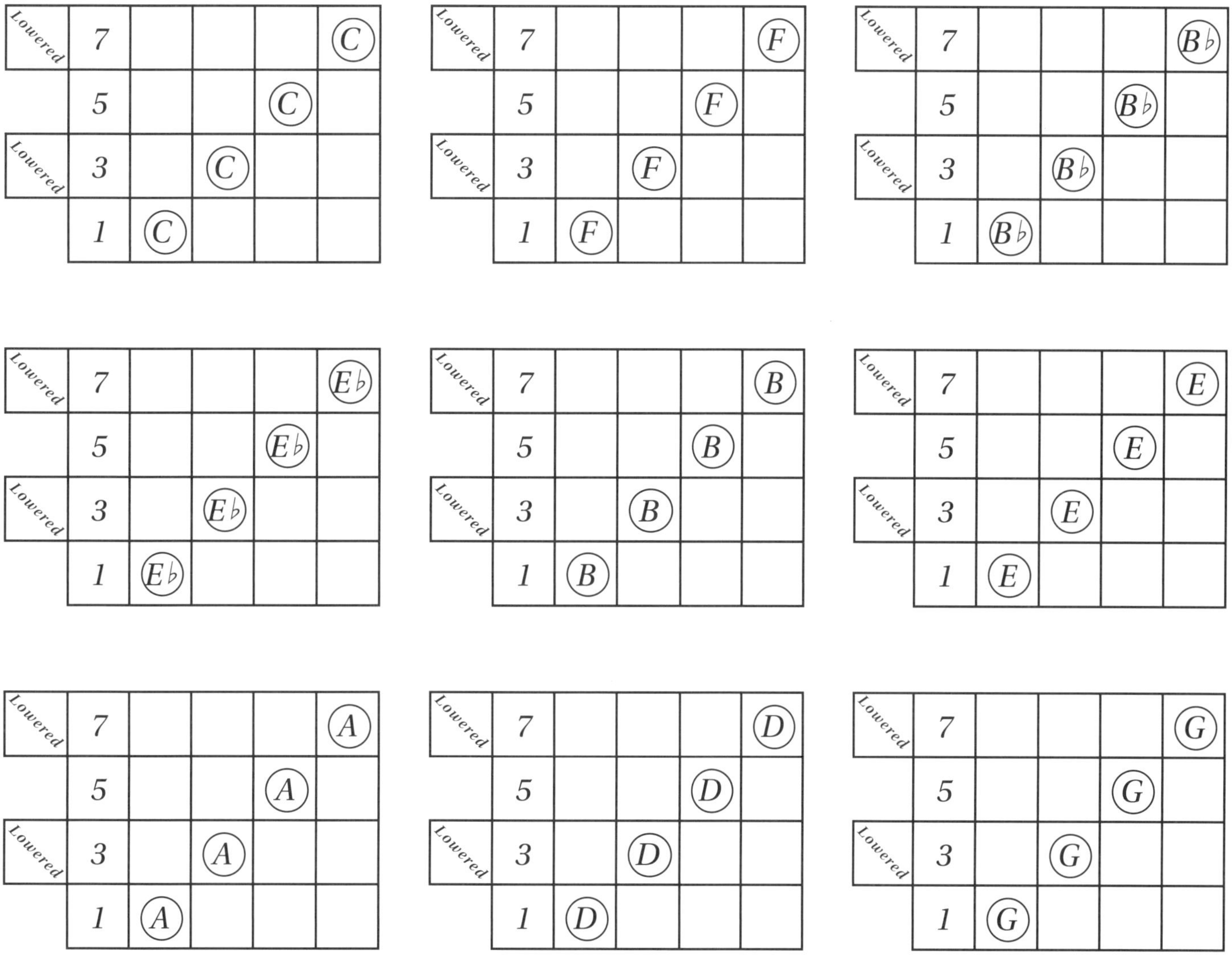

FIG. 3.21. Minor Seventh Chord Blocks

2. In order to have a convenient reference as you work, complete the enclosed chart. For each root, notate each chord type in all inversions.

FIG. 3.22. Chord Reference Chart

3. Convert the following closed chords to open position:

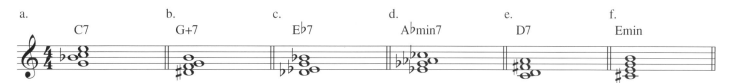

FIG. 3.23. Closed Chords

4. Set up harmonic continuities as described in lesson 2 on each of the following chord progressions. Do not allow the top note of any chord to go below the note E.

Where voice leading would result in a lower lead note, change the position of the previous chord.

FIG. 3.24. Continuity Practice: Sample

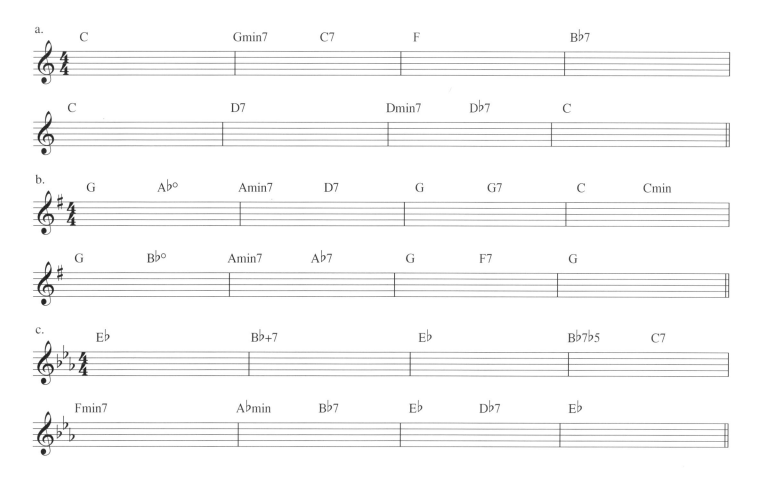

FIG. 3.25. Continuity Practice

5.   Rescore each of the continuities you have written in problem 7, as illustrated
     below.

FIG. 3.26. Rescoring Practice Sample

Notating Rhythms, Harmonizations

RHYTHM

For preparation in the development and usage of swing figures, we here analyze the rhythm factors that tend to produce a feeling of "swing."

First, let us consider the fact that a 4/4 bar contains eight eighth notes.

FIG. 4.1. Eighth Notes in a 4/4 Bar

Swing consists generally of a combination of accents in the above bar where at least one accent does not occur on the beat—i.e., one of the accents must occur on one of the "ands" (+) rather than directly on the 1, 2, 3, or 4.

a.

b.

c.

FIG. 4.2. Swing Examples

In order to avoid confusion in locating and naming "off-beat" attacks, we shall rely on a system of naming whereby every eighth note gets one beat. Using this system (i.e., eighth note gets one beat), the following durations may be represented by a single note:

NOTE	DURATION	EQUIVALENT REST
♪	1 Beat	⁊
♩	2 Beats	𝄽
♩.	3 Beats	𝄽⁊
𝅗𝅥	4 Beats	▬
𝅗𝅥.	6 Beats	▬ 𝄽
𝅝	8 Beats	▬

FIG. 4.3. Note Durations & Equivalent Rests

The rhythm "2 1 1 4" would appear as follows:

FIG. 4.4. 2 1 1 4 Notated

Following are several bars of rhythm, notated according to this method of naming:

FIG. 4.5. Notated Rhythm

Each bar should, of course, add up to eight "eighth" beats.

Whenever a duration cannot be represented by a single note, a "tie" is used to link two notes into one duration. The duration "5" might be indicated as:

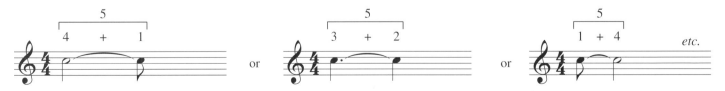

FIG. 4.6. Rhythm of 5 Notated

To illustrate further, the rhythm "5" plus "3" would be notated as follows:

FIG. 4.7. Rhythm 5 + 3

The rhythm "1" plus "2" plus "5" would be notated:

FIG. 4.8. Rhythm 1 + 2 + 5

The arranger, or composer, must follow a definite system of notation so that even the most intricate swing rhythms may be read easily and accurately. The three principles by which this may be accomplished are as follows:

1. A note, whether heard or not, should appear on the third beat of every 4/4 bar. This may be accomplished by simply picturing an *imaginary bar line* in the middle of the bar and only allowing four eighths (or their equivalent) to show on either side of it.

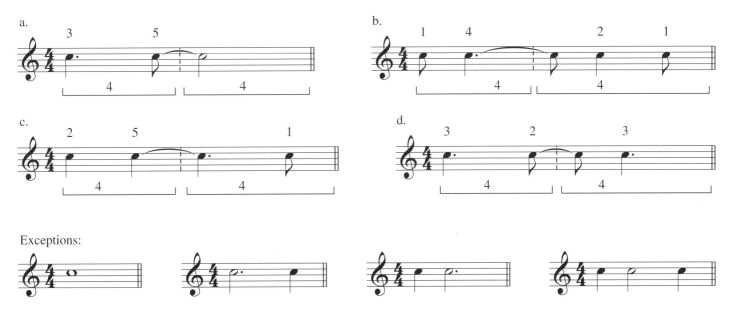

FIG. 4.9. Imaginary Bar Line

2. When two or more consecutive eighth notes occur in a group, they may be
    "beamed."

Beamed Eighth Notes

FIG. 4.10. Beamed Eighth Notes

However, do not "beam" eighth notes over the imaginary bar lines.

FIG. 4.11. Beamed Eighth Notes and the Imaginary Bar Line

3. Notes should always be spaced in the bar according to their valuation, i.e., a
    half note in a four-four bar should occupy one-half of the total space in the
    bar; a dotted half note should occupy three-fourths of the bar, etc.

FIG. 4.12. Note Spacing

Complete problems 1 and 2 of the lesson assignment. (See page 52.)

FOUR-PART HARMONIZATION OF A GIVEN MELODY

In this lesson, we come to what is certainly one of the most important techniques of arranging: how to harmonize a given melody in the modern "block" style. We will start out with a given melodic line with chord symbols and set up a four-part block harmonization suitable for adaption to any instrumental combination.

In past lessons, we have dealt exclusively with chord notes: notes contained in the given chord. When working with standard and popular tunes, however, we find that not all melody notes are simple chord notes. There, for the present, we may analyze any melody note according to one of the following classifications:

1. Chord Notes

2. Non-Chord Notes

In the following example, a melody with chord symbols is given and each note of the melody has been analyzed as either a chord note (c), or a non-chord note (nc).

FIG. 4.13. Melody with Chord Notes (c) and Non-Chord Notes (nc)

Before continuing with the lesson, it would be advisable to complete problem 3 of the assignment, page 53.

Once you are able to determine with little or no difficulty whether each note of the melody is a chord note or a non-chord note, the next step will be to fill out the chord under each and every note in "block style." Here are the rules for producing a four-part block harmonization.

1. Harmonize chord notes with the chord, building down from the melody note in the closest possible inversion.

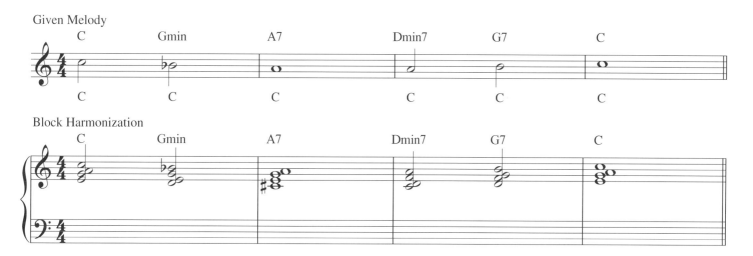

FIG. 4.14. Harmonization of Chord Notes

2. Harmonize non-chord notes with the chord, building down from the melody note in the closest possible inversion, but leaving out the nearest regular chord note just below the melody note.

For example, if we were harmonizing the note "B" with a Cmin chord (C, E♭, G, A), we would have to leave out the note "A" (the nearest chord note below "B") before filling in the rest of the chord notes.

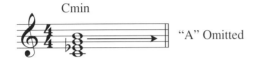

FIG. 4.15. A Omitted

Here are several more illustrations of the harmonization of non-chord notes.

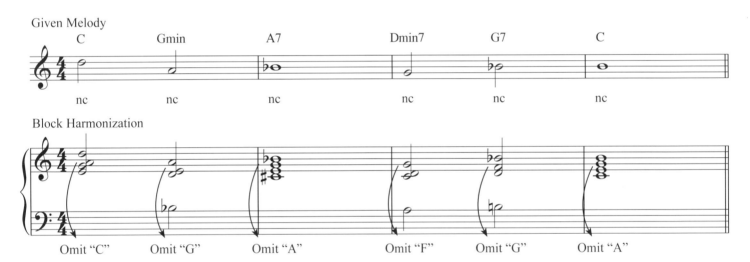

FIG. 4.16. Harmonization of Non-Chord Notes

Next, we move on to melodies which, like all standard and popular songs, will intermingle both chord and non-chord notes. Here is a melody of this sort complete with chord symbols, and an illustration of how it would be harmonized.

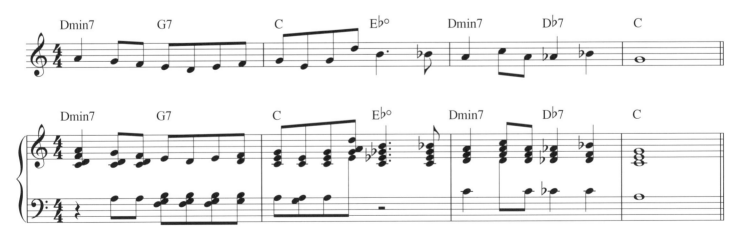

FIG. 4.17. Melody and Harmony Example

Remember that this same procedure may be followed in effectively harmonizing any of the standard or popular melodies with which you are familiar. If scored and orchestrated properly, the resulting harmonizations, while quite simple, would nevertheless produce the same professional sound featured by many leading bands.

In cases where the three lower voices do not change between chords, a smoother effect may be achieved by sustaining, rather than reattacking the notes. Remember that this applies only where each of the three lower voices would have repeated.

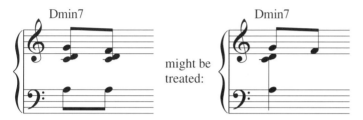

FIG. 4.18. Sustaining Notes

In the following illustration, the lower three voices cannot be sustained, since they actually change from one chord to the next.

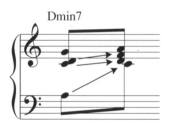

FIG. 4.19. All Notes Move

Another situation where the above principle might be applied would be where both the melody and the lower voices remain the same. Here, it would be possible to move only the top part while the three lower voices sustain.

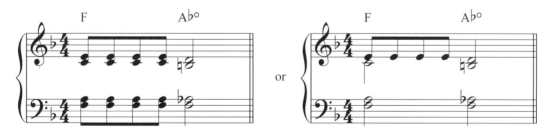

FIG. 4.20. Top Voice Moves

It would be wise to remember that regardless of how often this sustaining technique may be employed, it is far more effective in smooth ballads, rather than in "swing type" tunes. (It is also more generally used in saxes rather than in brass.)

ASSIGNMENT

1. Notate the following swing rhythms, as indicated in figure 4.21.

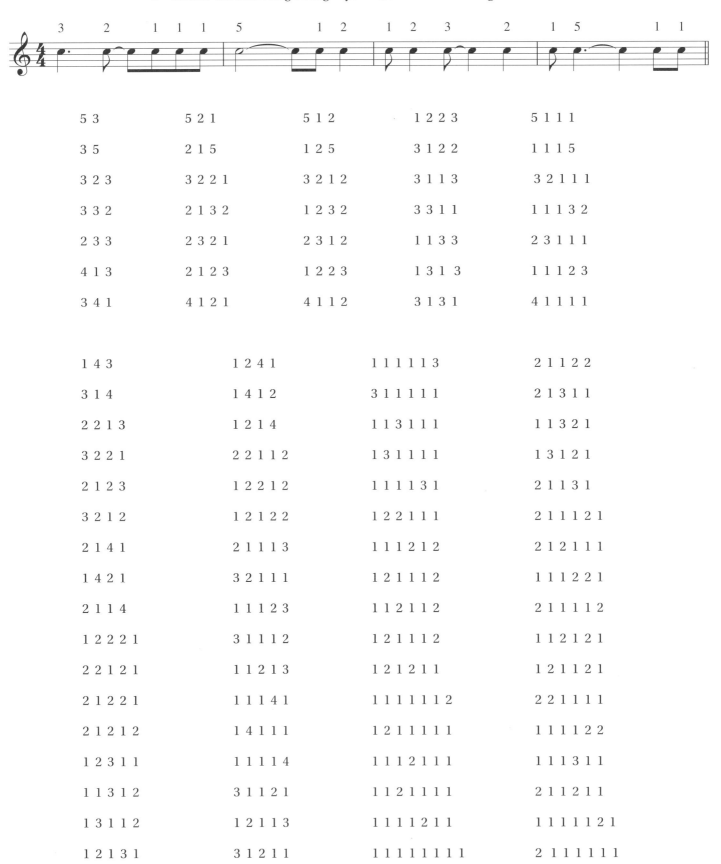

5 3	5 2 1	5 1 2	1 2 2 3	5 1 1 1
3 5	2 1 5	1 2 5	3 1 2 2	1 1 1 5
3 2 3	3 2 2 1	3 2 1 2	3 1 1 3	3 2 1 1 1
3 3 2	2 1 3 2	1 2 3 2	3 3 1 1	1 1 1 3 2
2 3 3	2 3 2 1	2 3 1 2	1 1 3 3	2 3 1 1 1
4 1 3	2 1 2 3	1 2 2 3	1 3 1 3	1 1 1 2 3
3 4 1	4 1 2 1	4 1 1 2	3 1 3 1	4 1 1 1 1

1 4 3	1 2 4 1	1 1 1 1 3	2 1 1 2 2	
3 1 4	1 4 1 2	3 1 1 1 1 1	2 1 3 1 1	
2 2 1 3	1 2 1 4	1 1 3 1 1 1	1 1 3 2 1	
3 2 2 1	2 2 1 1 2	1 3 1 1 1 1	1 3 1 2 1	
2 1 2 3	1 2 2 1 2	1 1 1 1 3 1	2 1 1 3 1	
3 2 1 2	1 2 1 2 2	1 2 2 1 1 1	2 1 1 1 2 1	
2 1 4 1	2 1 1 1 3	1 1 1 2 1 2	2 1 2 1 1 1	
1 4 2 1	3 2 1 1 1	1 2 1 1 1 2	1 1 1 2 2 1	
2 1 1 4	1 1 1 2 3	1 1 2 1 1 2	2 1 1 1 1 2	
1 2 2 2 1	3 1 1 1 2	1 2 1 1 1 2	1 1 2 1 2 1	
2 2 1 2 1	1 1 2 1 3	1 2 1 2 1 1	1 2 1 1 2 1	
2 1 2 2 1	1 1 1 4 1	1 1 1 1 1 1 2	2 2 1 1 1 1	
2 1 2 1 2	1 4 1 1 1	1 2 1 1 1 1 1	1 1 1 1 2 2	
1 2 3 1 1	1 1 1 1 4	1 1 1 2 1 1 1	1 1 1 3 1 1	
1 1 3 1 2	3 1 1 2 1	1 1 2 1 1 1 1	2 1 1 2 1 1	
1 3 1 1 2	1 2 1 1 3	1 1 1 1 2 1 1	1 1 1 1 1 2 1	
1 2 1 3 1	3 1 2 1 1	1 1 1 1 1 1 1 1	2 1 1 1 1 1 1	

FIG. 4.21. Rhythms for Notation Practice

2. In the following problem, rhythms employing rests will be used. Remember that the principles of bar-subdivision apply to rests as well as to durations.

FIG. 4.22. Rhythms with Rests

Notate the following swing rhythms:

a. 1, 1, 1, 2, (1,) 1, 2, 2, (4,) 1, 2, 1, 1, 1, 1, 1, 2, (5,) 1, 2, 2, 1, 1, (4,) 3, 1, 1, 1, 2, (2,) 4, 4, 2, (3.)

b. 2, (1,) 1, 1, 1, (1,) 2, 1, 1, 1, (1,) 1, 1, 2, 5, 1, 2, (5,) 1, 3, 1, 1, 1, 1, (1,) 3, 1, 1, 1, 2, 2, (2,) 1, 1, 1, (1,) 2, 1, 1, 1, (4.)

c. 7, 2, (6,) 1, 1, 1, 1, 1, 2, 1, 2, (2,) 2, 2, 1, 3, 2, (1,) 3, 3, 1, 1, 1, 1, (1,) 3, 1, 1, (1,) 1, 1, 1, 1, 2, (3.)

3. Analyze each of the following melodies indicating chord notes (C) and non-chord notes (NC).

FIG. 4.23. Label Each Note C (Chord Note) or NC (Non-Chord Note)

4. Harmonize each of the melodies from problem 3 using the four-part block technique described in this lesson. Sustain three lower voices wherever possible.

5. Write a four-part block harmonization on any two standard tunes of your choice.

Principles of Improvisation: Chord Tones, Approach Notes, and Chord Scales

CHORD TONES AND APPROACH NOTES

Notes of any given chord may be used in any order, frequency, or rhythm pattern against that chord.

FIG. 5.1. Chord Tones

Chromatic Approach Notes

Any note that chromatically approaches a chord tone may be used in an improvisation. These approach notes are always of short duration (a quarter note or less).

FIG. 5.2. Chromatic Approach Notes

Notice that in the foregoing example, each non-chord note chromatically approaches a regular chord note.

Scale-Wise Approach Notes

Any note that approaches a chord tone "scale-wise" may be used in an improvisation. (Scale-wise approaches must also be of short duration.)

CHORD SCALES

A prerequisite to understanding this technique of using approach notes is a knowledge of "chord scales."

Major (6 or 7)

In the case of the major chord, no alteration is necessary. The major scale, as is, goes with the major chord.

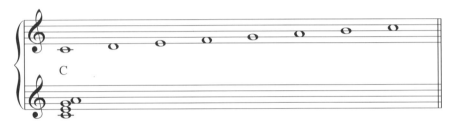

FIG. 5.3. Major Chord with Major Scale

A non-chord scale note may be used in an improvisation if it approaches an adjacent chord tone. Notice in the following example that every non-chord scale note moves directly into the nearest chord note (either above or below).

FIG. 5.4. Major Chord with Non-Chord Tones

Minor

Since the third degree is lowered in the minor chord, the same alteration will be made in the minor "chord scale."

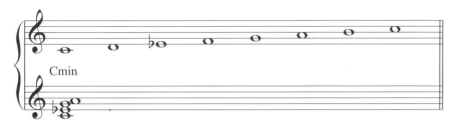

FIG. 5.5. Minor Chord Scale with Minor Chord

Again, here is an example of non-chord scale tones of the "minor chord scale" approaching adjacent chord tones.

FIG. 5.6. Non-Chord-Scale Tones of a Minor Chord Scale

Dominant 7

Here, the seventh degree is lowered in the chord scale just as it has been in the chord.

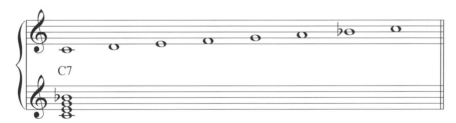

FIG. 5.7. Dominant Chord and C7 Chord Scale

Following is an example showing non-chord tones of the C7 chord scale moving into adjacent chord tones.

FIG. 5.8. Dominant 7 Chord with Non-Chord Tones

Minor 7

In the minor seventh chord, both the third and the seventh degrees are lowered. The same alterations have been made in the chord scale.

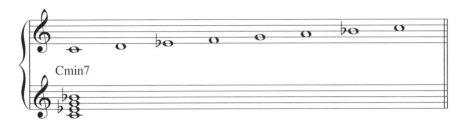

FIG. 5.9. C Minor Chord and Chord Scale

Every non-chord scale tone in the following example moves directly into the nearest chord tone.

FIG. 5.10. Non-Chord Scale Tones Moving to C Minor Chord Tones

Augmented 7

Here, the scale building procedure is slightly different. Instead of referring to, and altering, the basic major scale, we construct a "whole-tone" scale—i.e., a scale composed solely of whole-tone intervals.

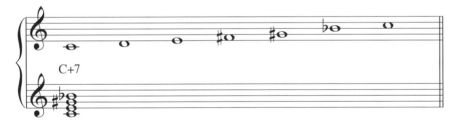

FIG. 5.11. C Augmented 7 Chord and Chord Scale

NOTE: This scale, necessarily, has only six notes (plus the added octave) instead of the usual seven.

Here is an example of scale-wise approaches into chord notes of the augmented seventh chord.

FIG. 5.12. Scale-Wise Approaches to Augmented Chord Tones

Diminished 7

Again, without referring to the basic major scale, we build the altered scale for the diminished seventh chord as follows: chord notes plus one whole step above each chord note.

FIG. 5.13. Diminished 7 Chord and Chord Scale

> **NOTE:** This scale will have eight notes (plus the added octave) rather than the usual seven.

Following is an example showing scale tones approaching adjacent chord tones of the diminished chord.

FIG. 5.14. Scale Tones Approaching Adjacent Diminished Chord Tones

> **NOTE:** When a minor 7♭5 structure is indicated, use the chord scale of the dominant 7 chord found four half steps below.

- Emin7♭5: use C7 chord scale
- Bmin7♭5: use G7 chord scale
- Fmin7♭5: use D♭7 chord scale

Typical mistakes in the use of approach notes are as follows.

In figure 5.15, although D♯ would be chromatic to a regular chord note of the C chord (E), in this case it cannot be considered to be a chromatic approach note since it is leaping into a chord note rather than approaching it chromatically.

FIG. 5.15. Approach by Leap

Similarly, the B♭ in figure 5.16 would be correct had it been followed by either C or A♭, but cannot be considered to be a scalewise approach to E♭. E♭ is *not an adjacent* chord note.

FIG. 5.16. Approach by Leap

In figure 5.17, F♯ would not be correct since it is neither a chromatic approach note nor is it present as a scale tone in the C scale.

FIG. 5.17. Neither Chromatic Approach nor Scale Tone

NOTE: Although the foregoing will produce excellent musical results in virtually every situation, this should not be considered as a final and complete coverage of scale-chord relationships. In some cases, the scale will be determined not by the structure of the chord, but by its function in the overall tonality of the chord sequence. This will be covered in more detail in the section of the course dealing with chord progression.

IMPROVISATION

The ability to "ad lib"—to improvise around a given melody, or to create an original melodic improvisation on a chord progression—is as essential to the arranger as it is to the instrumentalist.

Creating an Original Improvisation On a Chord Progression

1. **Chord Notes.** As stated earlier in this lesson, chord notes may be freely used in creating original melodies.

FIG. 5.18. Chord Tones as Melody

2. **Chromatic Approach Notes.** Chromatic approach notes may precede any regular chord note provided that they resolve directly to that chord note.

FIG. 5.19. Chromatic Approach Notes in a Melody

3. **Scalewise Approach Notes.** Non-chord notes that are present in the related chord scale may be used, provided that they resolve directly into an adjacent chord note and are of short duration.

FIG. 5.20. Scalewise Approach Notes

Following is an example of an original melody based on a given chord progression that utilizes:

1. Chord tones

2. Chromatic approach notes

3. Scalewise approach notes

IMPORTANT: *All approach notes must be of short duration.*

Quarter notes that occur on the first or third beat should not normally be harmonized as approach notes.

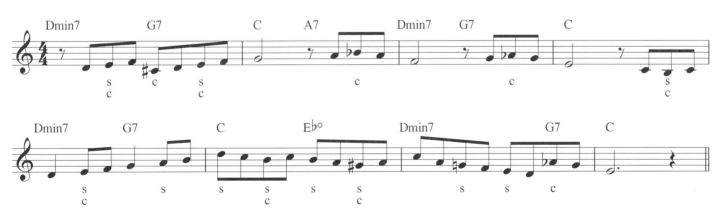

FIG. 5.21. Melody with Chord Notes, Scalewise Approach Notes, and Chromatic Approach Notes

To be certain that the foregoing is perfectly clear, here, once again, is an original melody composed exclusively of those materials covered in this lesson.

FIG. 5.22. Melody with Chord Notes, Scalewise Approach Notes, and Chromatic Approach Notes

ASSIGNMENT

1. Write out chord scales on each of the following notes as shown in figure 5.23:
   C, D♭, D, E♭, E, F, F♯, G, A♭, A, B♭, B.

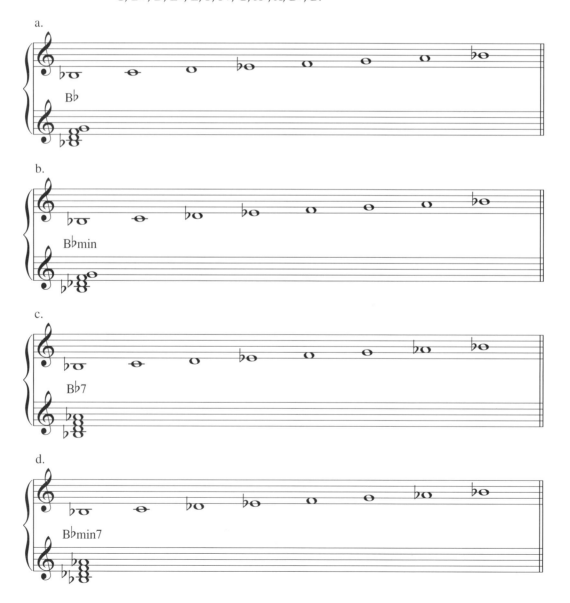

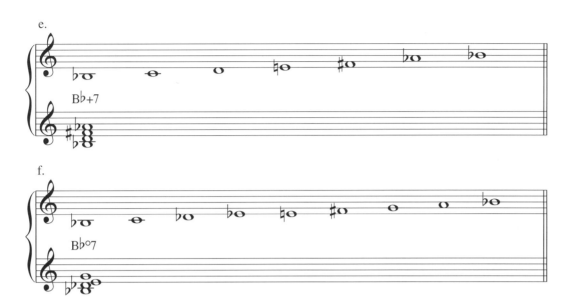

FIG. 5.23. Chord Scale Practice

2. In the event that you do have access to a piano, it is definitely advisable to spend some time playing and listening to the chord scales discussed in this lesson. The most effective way is to sustain the closed chord in the left hand while playing the altered scale in the right. Remember that speed is not essential, but attentive listening is.

   (Play all chord scales notated in problem 1.)

3. Using only chord notes, chromatic approach notes, and scalewise approach notes, compose original improvisations based on each of the following chord progressions:

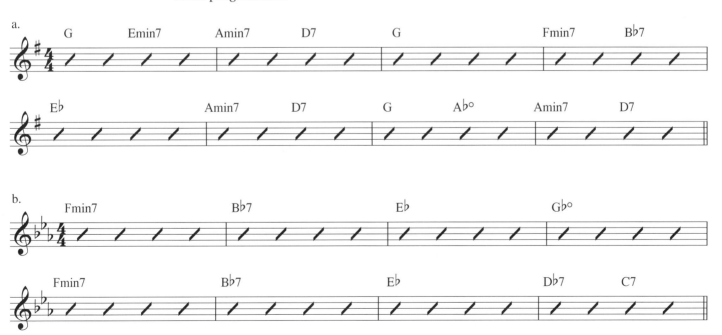

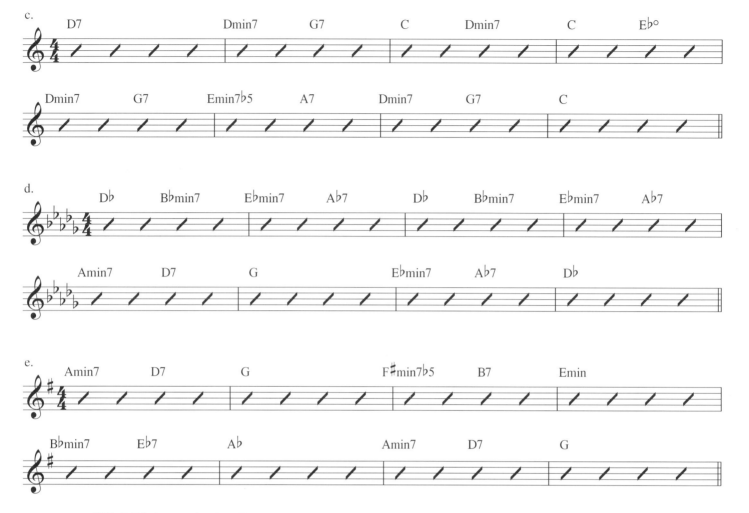

FIG. 5.24. Improvisation Practice

4. Using each of the following chord progressions as a guide, set up a four-stave score as illustrated in figure 5.25.

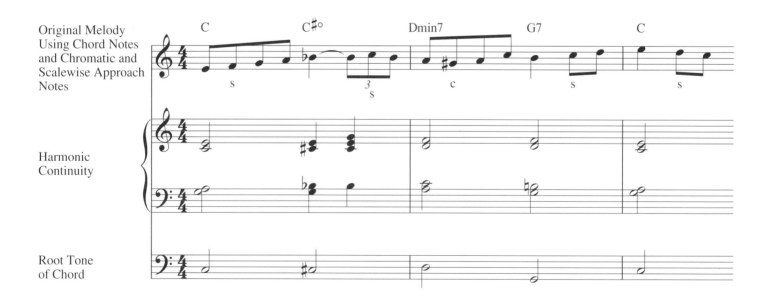

FIG. 5.25. Arranging Practice

5. Write a four-part harmonization of each of the following melodies:

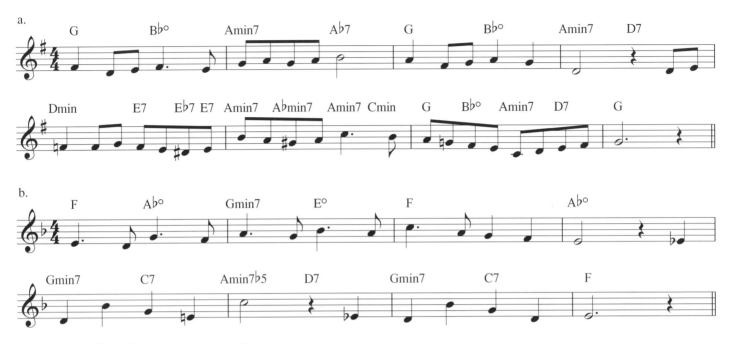

FIG. 5.26. Harmonization Practice

6. Write a four-part harmonization in open position of each of the following melodies:

FIG. 5.27. Harmonization Practice: Open Position

Improvisation: Delayed Resolution and Rhythmic Displacement

In lesson 5, we covered some of the melodic elements to be considered in improvising. We continue now with some melodic figurations that may be effectively used.

DELAYED RESOLUTION

In a *delayed resolution*, the chord note is approached from both above and below before resolution occurs. The delayed resolution may take either of the following forms:

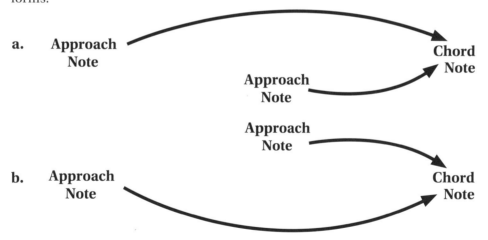

FIG. 6.1. Delayed Resolution

Following are some typical examples of delayed resolutions.

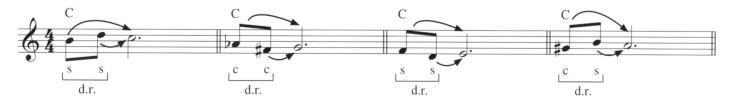

FIG. 6.2. Delayed Resolution Examples

DOUBLE CHROMATIC APPROACH

A *double chromatic approach* is a melodic figuration consisting of two chromatic notes moving in the same direction into the chord tone. The double chromatic approach almost always assumes one of the following forms:

FIG. 6.3. Double Chromatic Approach Examples

Figure 6.4 is an example of an original melody created from a given chord progression using all of the techniques of melodic improvisation that have been discussed in lessons 5 and 6. Each note used has been coded as follows:

Chord Notes	|
Chromatic Approach Notes	c
Scalewise Approach Notes	s
Delayed Resolution	d.r.
Double Chromatic Approach	d.c.

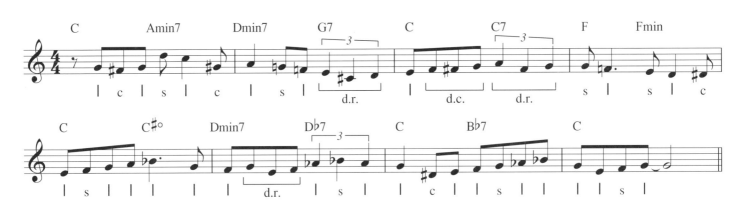

FIG. 6.4. Melody Based on Chord Progression

There are, of course, endless melodic variations that could be developed from this same series of chords. Following is another melody based on the chord progression given in figure 6.4.

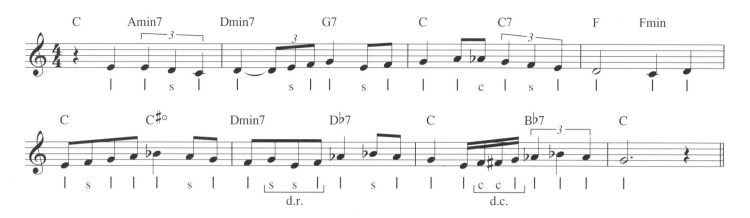

FIG. 6.5. Another Melody on the Same Progression

IMPROVISATION ON A GIVEN MELODY

The preceding has dealt with the construction of an original melody from a given chord progression. These same principles are in continual use by the instrumentalist or arranger. He has, however, the additional problem of writing a melodic variation (improvisation) on an already established melody.

In improvising on a given tune, it is normally advisable that the original melody be recognizable. The type of band or combo for which you happen to be playing or writing should be your guide in determining just how far from the original melody you dare to go.

All of the melodic techniques discussed in lessons 5 and 6 (i.e., chord notes, chromatic approach notes, scalewise approach notes, delayed resolutions, double chromatic approaches) may be applied to a given melody. Of course, in order that the original melody remain recognizable, notes of the original melody should be retained, especially those notes that are important in feeling or duration.

Notice in the following examples that the characteristics of the original melodies (a) have been kept in each of the improvisations (b). In addition to the coding described previously, notes of the original melody will now be indicated by "M."

NOTE: Quarter notes that occur on the first or third beat should not normally be harmonized as approach notes.

a. Original Melody 1

b. Improvisation 1

a. Original Melody 2

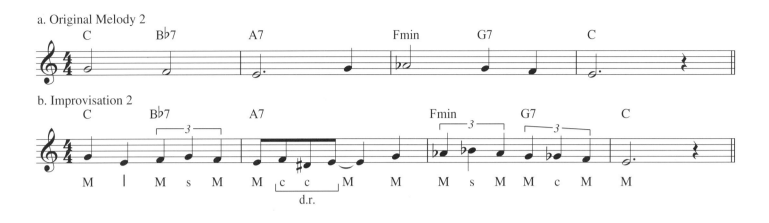

b. Improvisation 2

a. Original Melody 3

b. Improvisation 3

FIG. 6.6. Improvisation Based on Three Melodies

RHYTHM VARIATIONS

Any rhythmic pattern may assume a number of different forms and feelings depending upon its relative location in the bar. To illustrate, the simple rhythm "4 plus 4" might be used in any of the following ways:

(**NOTE:** 1 = eighth note.)

FIG. 6.7. Rhythmic Variations of 4 4

Rhythmic Displacement

To develop an understanding and awareness of the various forms that may be evolved from any rhythm pattern, we use the technique of "rhythmic displacement."

Displacement by an Eighth Note

In the following example, the pre-selected rhythmic pattern will be repeated eight times, but before each repetition an eighth rest will be inserted. As a result of this, the rhythm which begins on the first beat of the first bar will begin on the second beat of the next bar, the third beat of the following bar, etc., until the original rhythm pattern has been displaced one full bar.

Original Rhythm "1, 1, 1, 5"

FIG. 6.8. Rhythmic Displacement of 1 1 1 5 by an Eighth Note

It is, of course, possible to apply this same technique to rhythmic patterns that encompass any number of beats. In figure 6.9, a two-bar (sixteen eighth-note beats) rhythm pattern has been displaced by an eighth rest until it returns to its original form.

Original Rhythm "2, 2, 3, 2, 2, 1, 2, 2"

FIG. 6.9. Rhythmic Displacement of a Two-Bar Pattern

Displacement by Three Eighth Notes

The technique of rhythmic displacement remains the same except that a rest of three eighth-note beats is inserted before repeating the rhythm pattern.

(**NOTE:** In working with rests, be sure to use the same type of bar subdivision that you would in working with notes.)

Original Rhythm "2, 1, 1, 1, 3"

FIG. 6.10. Displacement by Three Eighth Notes

Next, a two-bar rhythmic pattern displaced by three eighth notes.

Original Rhythm "3, 4, 2, 2, 1, 1, 1, 2"

FIG. 6.11. Displacement of a Two-Bar Rhythmic Pattern by Three Eighth Notes

The value of rhythmic exercises of this sort cannot be stressed too strongly. Completion of the assigned problems will familiarize you with the type of rhythm, which is an essential part of modern music and jazz.

NOTES REGARDING THE USE OF TRIPLETS IN 4/4 TIME

Quarter-note triplets may begin only on the first or third beats of the bar.

FIG. 6.12. Quarter-Note Triplets in 4/4

Eighth-note triplets may begin on the first, second, third, or fourth beats of the bar only.

FIG. 6.13. Eighth-Note Triplets

NOTATION OF DOUBLE-TIME RHYTHMS

Double-time (i.e., the feeling of eight pulsations to the bar in 4/4 time) rhythms may be notated properly by observing the following:

1. Consider four subdivisions to the bar instead of the customary two.

FIG. 6.14. Subdividing a 4/4 Measure for Double-Time

2. Reduce each value of the original 4/4 rhythmic pattern by one-half, i.e., quarter note becomes an eighth note; dotted half becomes a dotted quarter; two bars become one bar, etc.

3. Beam each group of notes that occupy one-quarter beat of double-time (i.e., two beats of regular 4/4 time).

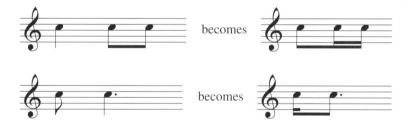

FIG. 6.15. Double-Time Durations

Following are several examples of rhythmic phrases (a) as they appear in 4/4 time; and (b) as they would be notated if a "double-time" feeling were desired.

FIG. 6.16. Double-Time Examples

NOTE: Double-time is used exclusively in slow and medium-slow tempos.

ASSIGNMENT

1. Given are some chord progressions. (Figure 6.18)

   a. Write harmonic continuities based on these progressions.

   b. Improvise original melodies on the chord progressions. Remember that there must be an explanation for each and every note used. (See figures 6.4 and 6.5).

   c. Code each note similar to figures 6.4 and 6.5.

FIG. 6.17. Sample Solution

FIG. 6.18. Practice Progressions

2. Given are some original melodies with chord symbols. (Figure 6.20)

    a. Write harmonic continuities in open position based on the chord
        progressions.

    b. Write an improvised variation of each of these melodies. (Important:
        Original melody must be recognizable).

    c. Code each note as in figure 6.6b.

FIG. 6.19. Sample Solution

FIG. 6.20. Given Melodies

3. Displace each of the following rhythmic patterns by an eighth note. Continue until the pattern returns to its original form.

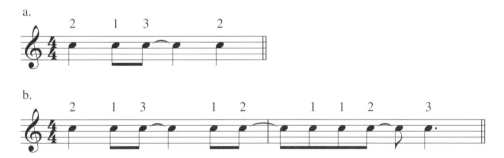

FIG. 6.21. Patterns for Rhythmic Displacement Practice

4. Displace each of the following rhythmic patterns by three eighth notes. Continue until the pattern returns to its original form.

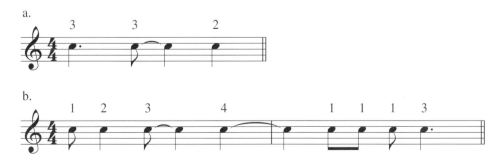

FIG. 6.22. Patterns for Rhythmic Displacement Practice

5. Convert each of the rhythmic continuities resulting from problem 3 to double-time. Remember that each of the phrases will be reduced to half as many bars as the original.

LESSON 7

Modern Block Harmonization

MELODIC ANALYSIS

Before attempting to harmonize a melodic line in the manner to be discussed, it is important to understand the function of each note of the melody.

We may start by assuming that every note of a melody must fall into one of the following classifications.

1. Chord Notes: notes belonging to the chord indicated above the melodic line.

FIG. 7.1. Chord Notes

2. Non-Chord, Non-Approach Notes: non-chord notes that do not function as approach notes.

FIG. 7.2. Non-Chord Notes

Since one of the conditions relating to approach notes stipulates that they must be of short duration, we may assume that any non-chord note more than one quarter beat in duration would automatically fall into this classification.

FIG. 7.3. Chord Notes Are Longer than a Quarter Note

3. Scalewise Approach Notes (see lesson 5)

FIG. 7.4. Scalewise Approach Notes

4. Chromatic Approach Notes (see lesson 5)

FIG. 7.5. Chromatic Approach Notes

In addition to the regular chromatic approaches discussed in lesson 5, notes that are classified as non-chord, non-approach may also be approached chromatically.

FIG. 7.6. Chromatic Non-Chord, Non-Approach Notes

In the following example, each note of the given melody has been appropriately coded as follows:

Chord Notes |
Non-Chord, Non-Approach Notes   nc
Scalewise Approach Notes   s
Chromatic Approach Notes   c

FIG. 7.7. Analyzed Melody

In certain instances, more than one possibility for analysis exists. In these cases, the most desirable choice has been noted. Where an approach note may be classified as either scalewise or chromatic, it is usually (but not always) advisable to treat it as a scalewise approach.

As you complete the block harmonization of the assigned melodies, it is advisable that you play each of the possible harmonizations wherever a choice exists so that you may select the one that sounds best to you.

(At this point, complete problems 1 and 2 of the assignment.)

MODERN BLOCK HARMONIZATION PROCEDURES

Once each note of the melodic line has been properly analyzed, the actual harmonization becomes a relatively simple procedure.

1. Chord Notes. Harmonize chord notes with the designated chord (as in four-part harmonization, see lesson 4).

FIG. 7.8. Harmonize Chord Notes

2. Non-Chord, Non-Approach Notes. Harmonize non-chord, non-approach notes with the chord, omitting the nearest chord note just below the lead.

FIG. 7.9. Harmonize Non-Chord, Non-Approach Notes

3. Scalewise Approach Notes. Harmonize scalewise approach notes with the diminished chord of the note being harmonized.

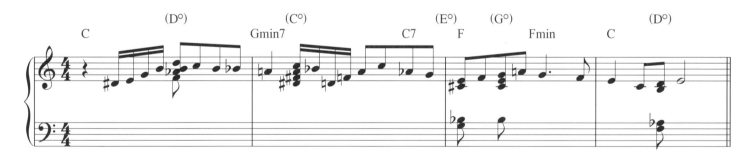

FIG. 7.10. Harmonize Scalewise Approach Notes

4. Chromatic Approach Notes. Harmonize chromatic approach notes chromatically in all voices. (Each note moves chromatically in the same direction into its adjacent chord note.)

FIG. 7.11. Harmonize Chromatic Approach Notes

The completed harmonization would appear as follows:

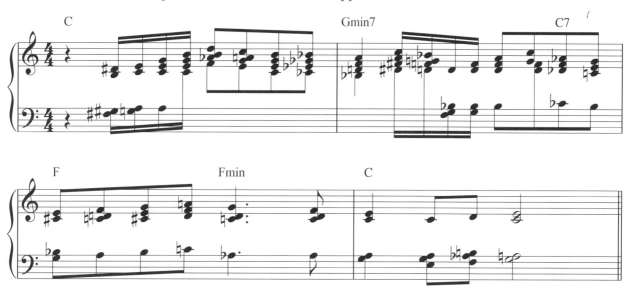

FIG. 7.12. Completed Harmonization

Following is an illustration of the modern block harmonization of a given melody. In figure 7.13, the analysis has been made and each note coded.

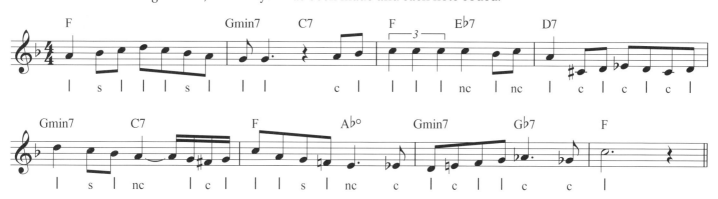

FIG. 7.13. Analyzed Melody for Block Harmonization

In figure 7.14, the harmonization of the melody in figure 7.13 is actually completed.

FIG. 7.14. Harmonization of Melody in Figure 7.13

Reminder: Quarter notes that occur on the first or third beat should not normally be harmonized as approach notes. It is important that the chord sound be heard on these strong beats, when the attack lasts for a full beat or more.

Just to be certain that the foregoing is perfectly clear, here is another example employing the techniques described in this lesson.

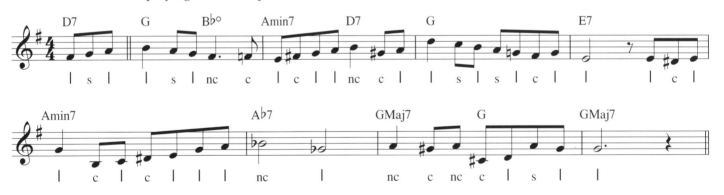

FIG. 7.15. Analyzed Melody for Block Harmonization

Here is the harmonization of the melody in figure 7.15.

FIG. 7.16. Harmonization of Melody in Figure 7.15

ASSIGNMENT

1. Analyze and code each of the following melodies (see figure 7.7).

FIG. 7.17. Practice Melodies

2. In a similar manner, analyze and code any three standard tunes of your
    choice.

3. Write a modern block harmonization of each of the melodies given in
    problem 1.

4. Write a modern block harmonization of each of the standard tunes analyzed
    in problem 2.

Rhythmic Anticipation and Additional Harmonization Techniques

RHYTHMIC ANTICIPATION

In lesson 4, we discussed those factors that tend to produce a feeling of swing and also the methods of notating these swing rhythms correctly. In this lesson, we cover *rhythmic anticipation*—a technique whereby we may take any simple tune and alter it rhythmically so that it "swings."

The rule for using rhythmic anticipation is as follows:

Notes on the beat may be anticipated by attacking them an eighth beat sooner than they originally occur.

FIG. 8.1. Adding Rhythmic Anticipation

Although in the preceding example, rhythmic anticipation has been used wherever possible, in actual usage, anticipation is most effective when alternated with occasional "on-the-beat" attacks (see figure 8.2b).

Following is an improvisation of the melody given in figure 8.1 utilizing rhythmic anticipation to produce swing feeling.

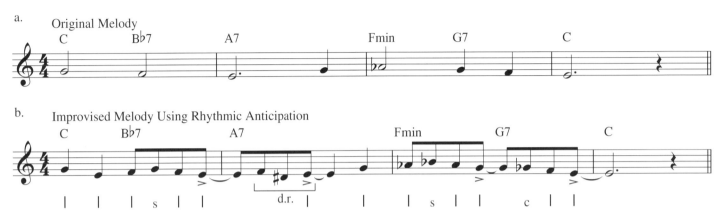

FIG. 8.2. Adding Rhythmic Anticipation

MODERN BLOCK HARMONIZATION (CONT.)

Harmonization of Rhythmic Anticipation

When working out the block harmonization of a note that has been rhythmically anticipated, be sure to anticipate the harmony as well as the melody.

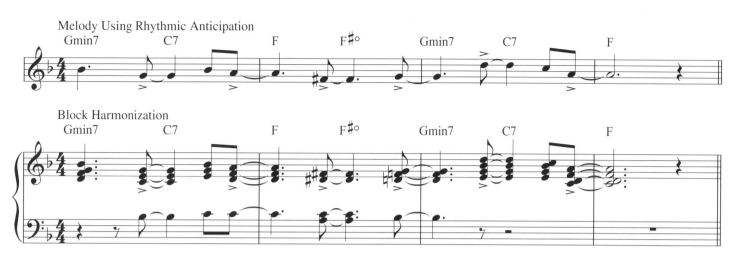

FIG. 8.3. Adding Rhythmic Anticipation to a Block Harmonization I

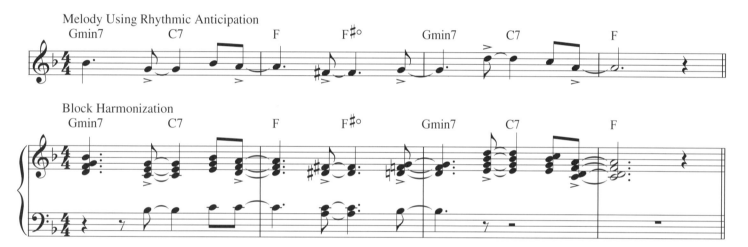

FIG. 8.4. Adding Rhythmic Anticipation to a Block Harmonization II

Notice in the preceding examples that the chord symbols still appear over the first or third beats of the bar even though the melody and the block harmony have been anticipated.

Harmonization of the Double-Chromatic Approach

Harmonize each of the chromatic approaches so that all voices move chromatically into the following chord. (See lesson 6.)

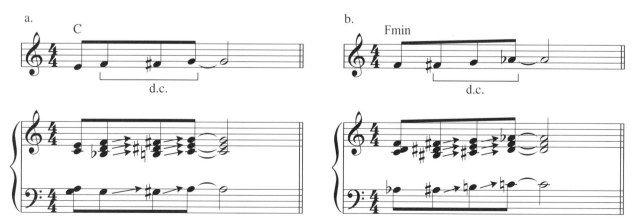

FIG. 8.5. Harmonization of the Double-Chromatic Approach

Harmonization of the Delayed Resolve

Harmonize each approach note of the delayed resolve as though the other approach did not exist. (See lesson 6.)

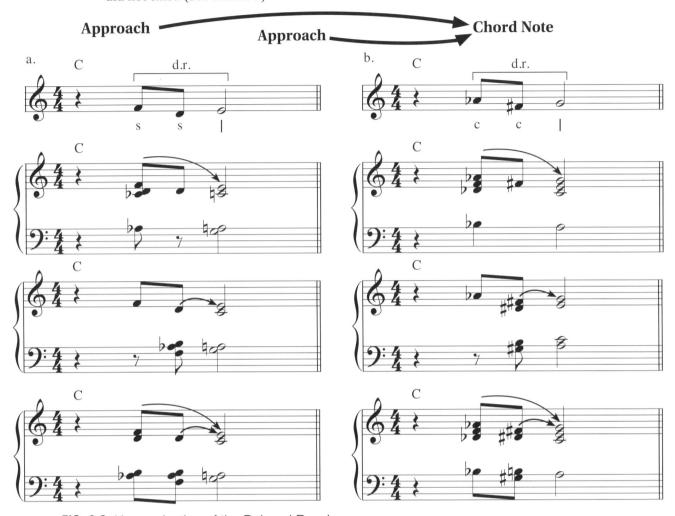

FIG. 8.6. Harmonization of the Delayed Resolve

Alteration of the Dominant 7 Chord

The following principle relating to the dominant 7 chord may be effectively used in modern block harmonization.

1. In any dominant 7 chord, the 9 may be substituted for 1—except when 1 is the melody note.

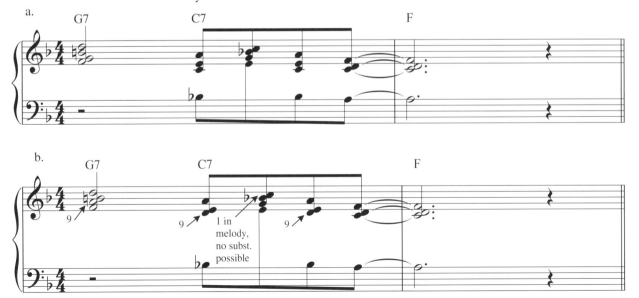

FIG. 8.7. Alteration of the Dominant 7 Chord in a Harmonization

2. Where a dominant 7 chord immediately precedes the tonic (i.e., V7 to I), the 9 may be lowered one half step in the dominant 7 chord.

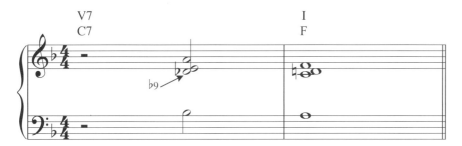

FIG. 8.8. Lowering the 9 when V7 Precedes I

3. With 1 in the lead of the V7 chord, the following alternate voicing may be used:

FIG. 8.9. Alternative Voicing for ♭9 with V7

Following is a reference chart showing the V7 to I cadence in every key. A detailed discussion of harmonic progression including all forms of cadence will be presented later in the course.

V7 to I
G7 to C
C7 to F
F7 to B♭
B♭7 to E♭
E♭7 to A♭
A♭7 to D♭
D♭7 to G♭
F♯7 to B
B7 to E
E7 to A
A7 to D
D7 to G

FIG. 8.10. "V7 to I" Cadence Chart

Following is an example of modern block harmonization that contains all of the new principles described in this lesson, as well as those covered in lesson 7.

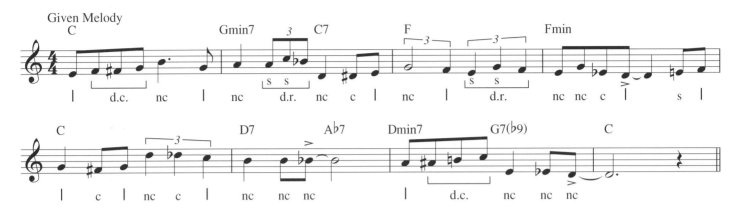

FIG. 8.11. Harmonization Example with Lesson 8 Principles

It is important that you study these examples closely, being certain that you understand each and every step in the harmonization procedure. Remember that your relative success or failure in successfully completing the lesson assignments depends upon your understanding of these examples.

HARMONIZATION OF IMPROVISED MELODIES

All of the techniques described in lessons 7 and 8 apply not only to the harmonization of given standard or popular tunes, but to the harmonization of improvised melodies as well. Here is an example showing the modern block harmonization of an improvised melody. All techniques employed in creating the improvisation have been discussed in lessons 5 and 6.

FIG. 8.12. Harmonization of an Improvised Melody

Necessarily, the preceding examples and illustrations have dealt with extreme applications of the special cases relating to improvisation and block harmonization. In actual usage, however, the best treatment is very often the simplest, with special cases such as the delayed resolve and the double chromatic approach used only for occasional effect.

Remember, also, that the best block harmonizations are usually a combination of modern block harmonization, and simple four-part harmonization as described in lesson 4.

OPEN VOICING OF MODERN BLOCK HARMONIZATION

Open position, as explained in lesson 3, may be effectively used in modern block harmonization. The technique remains the same:

Open position may be produced by dropping the second voice (from the top) down one octave.

Here is an illustration of modern block harmonization in open position.

FIG. 8.13. Harmonizations with Closed and Open Voicings

ASSIGNMENT

1. Write a modern block harmonization to each of the following melodies. Be sure to treat all rhythmic anticipations as illustrated in figure 8.3.

FIG. 8.14. Practice Melodies

2. Using the techniques described in lessons 5 and 6, write an improvised variation of each of the following melodies. Use rhythmic anticipation to produce a swing feeling in each of the improvisations.

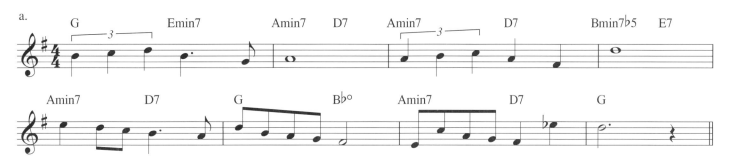

FIG. 8.15. Practice Melodies

3. Complete a modern block harmonization of each of the improvised melodies created in figure 8.15.

4. Using any standard or popular tune of your choice, complete the following problem:

    a. Write an improvised variation of the original melody. (Original melody must be recognizable.)

    b. Complete a modern block harmonization of the improvised melody.

5. Once again, using any given tune as a starting point, complete the following problem:

    a. Write an improvised variation of the original melody. Improvise as little or as much as you please, but in any event, the original melody must be identifiable.

    b. Complete a modern block harmonization of the improvised melody in open position.

Tensions

CHORD TENSIONS

In this lesson, we begin our discussion of *tensions*: high-degree chordal functions. These high-degree chordal functions are treated, for our purposes, just the same as chord notes, and have the same properties as those regular low-degree chord notes already discussed.

It is also interesting to note, at this time, that all of the so-called "non-chord, non-approach notes" that we encountered in modern block harmonization, are in reality high-degree chordal functions (i.e., tensions).

Locating these tensions may be simplified by recognizing that every high-degree chord note is located one whole step above a related low-degree chord note.

Following is a listing of practical tensions. In each case, the related low-degree chord note has been indicated.

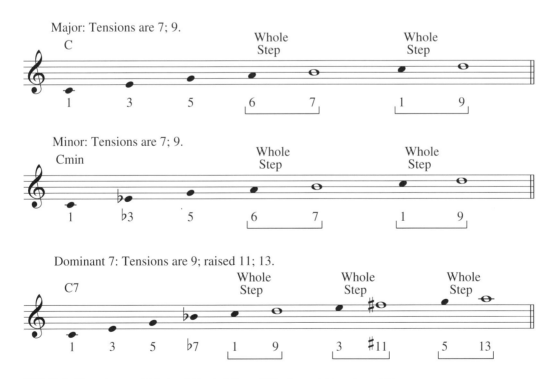

FIG. 9.1. Tensions of Major Triad, Minor Triad, and Dominant 7

[**NOTE:** Today, Berklee considers the 7 a basic chord tone, rather than a tension.—Ed.]

The scale 11 (located one-half step above the third) is also commonly used with dominant 7 chords. There are specific instances where this scale 11 is more effective than the raised 11 and vice versa. For the time being, experiment with both, and let your taste govern your choice.

Dominant 7: Scale 11

Minor 7: Tensions are 9; scale 11.

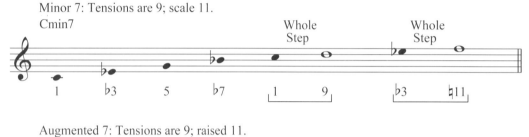

Augmented 7: Tensions are 9; raised 11.

Diminished 7: Tensions are one whole step above every low degree chord note.

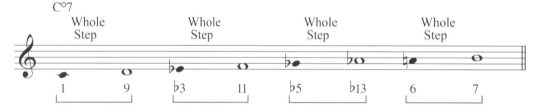

FIG. 9.2. Tension 11

(At this point, it would be advisable to complete problem 1 of the lesson assignment.)

As previously noted, we can now specifically identify those notes, which formerly had been classified simply as "non-chord, non-approach." In the analysis of the following melody, this general classification has been eliminated, and each of the tensions specifically named. Notice that this does not in any way affect the identification of those notes of the melody, which could be treated as approach notes.

Chord Notes	|
Tensions	by name
Scalewise Approach Notes	s
Chromatic Approach Notes	c

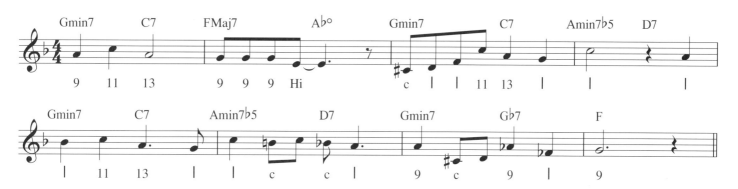

FIG. 9.3. Analysis of Tensions within a Melody

BLOCK HARMONIZATION OF TENSIONS

Those notes that we now call "tensions" are still harmonized the same as they were when classified as non-chord, non-approach: omit the related low-degree chord note just below the lead.

The following table may be used in checking the harmonization of any tension.

Major Triad			Minor Triad	
7	9	9	7	9
5	6	7	5	6
3	5	5	♭3	5
1	3	3	1	♭3
Dominant 7			**Minor 7**	
9	♯11	13	9	11
♭7	9*	3	♭7	1
5	♭7	9*	5	♭7
3	5	♭7	♭3	5
Augmented 7			**Diminished 7**			
9	♯11		9	11	♭13	7
♭7	9		♭♭7	1	♭3	♭5
♯5	♭7		♭5	♭♭7	1	♭3
3	♯5		♭3	♭5	♭♭7	1
			(Omit related low-degree chord note)			

FIG. 9.4. Chords and Tensions. *indicates 9 for 1 substitution in dominant 7 chords.

Figure 9.4 in musical notation would appear as follows:

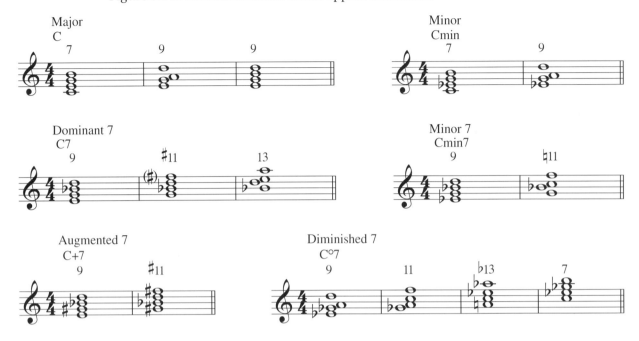

FIG. 9.5. Tensions of C Chords

Here is a modern block harmonization of the given melody analyzed in figure 9.3.

FIG. 9.6. Harmonization of Melody in Figure 9.3

TENSION-RESOLVE (HI-LO)

Although they do not always do so, there is a strong tendency for every tension to resolve to the related low degree chord note found one whole step below. Technically, this is known as "tension-resolve," or more simply "Hi-Lo" (i.e., "Hi" degree resolving to "Lo" degree.)

Following is an illustration showing all of the possibilities for Hi-Lo with each of the basic chord structures.

Major: 7 to 6; 9 to 1

Minor: 7 to 6; 9 to 1

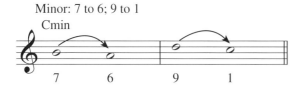

Dominant 7: 9 to 1; 11 (Scale or Raised) to 3; 13 to 5

Minor 7: 9 to 1; Scale 11 to ♭3

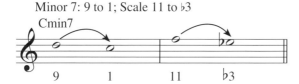

Augmented 7: 9 to 1; Raised 11 to 3

Diminished 7: One whole step above any chord note resolving down
to the related low degree chord note

FIG. 9.7. Hi-Lo of Basic Chord Types

Here is an example showing how an original theme might be composed using only Hi-Lo. The resulting sound should give you some idea of the value of having a good working knowledge of these tension-resolve patterns.

FIG. 9.8. Analyzed Melody with Tension-Resolve/Hi-Lo

HARMONIZATION OF HI-LO

Since the harmonization of both the tension and its related low-degree call for the same lower voices, any Hi-Lo may be harmonized by simply sustaining the three lower voices while the lead moves.

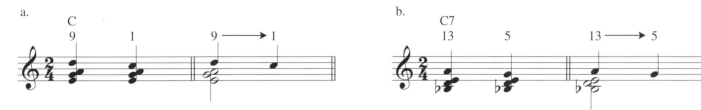

FIG. 9.9. Harmonizing Hi-Lo

The following table may be used in checking the harmonization of any tension-resolve pattern.

Major Triad		Minor Triad	
7→6 9→1		7→6 9→1	
5	6	5	6
3	5	♭3	5
1	3	1	♭3
Dominant 7			**Minor 7**		
9→1	♯11→3	13→5	9→1	11→♭3	
♭7	9	3	♭7	1	
5	♭7	9	5	♭7	
3	5	♭7	♭3	5	
Augmented 7			**Diminished 7**		
9→1	♯11→3		11→♭3	♭13→♭5	7→♭♭7
♭7	9		1	♭3	♭5
♯5	♭7		♭♭7	1	♭3
3	♯5		♭5	♭♭7	1

FIG. 9.10. Tension/Resolve (Hi-Lo) Patterns

To be certain that the foregoing is perfectly clear, here is figure 9.10 in musical notation.

FIG. 9.11. Tension/Resolve Patterns in C Chords

Utilizing the foregoing principles, the harmonization of figure 9.8 would appear as follows:

FIG. 9.12. Hi-Lo Harmonizations of Figure 9.8

An alternate technique used in the harmonization of tension-resolve is as follows: Two simultaneous Hi-Lo's may be used, provided that they are separated by the interval of a third.

This "double Hi-Lo" would appear as follows:

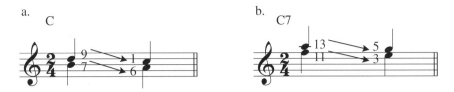

FIG. 9.13. Double Hi-Lo

The following illustration would be incorrect, since the Hi-Lo's are not separated by the interval of a third.

FIG. 9.14. Incorrect: Not Separated by a Third

Harmonization of tension-resolve using "double Hi-Lo" (only practical cases).

Major Triad		Minor Triad	
9→1		9→1	
7→6		7→6	
5		5	
3		♭3	
Dominant 7		**Minor 7**	
11→3	13→5	11→♭3	
9→1	11→3	9→1	
♭7	9	♭7	
5	♭7	5	

FIG. 9.15. Double Hi-Lo

Figure 9.15 in musical notation would have the following appearance:

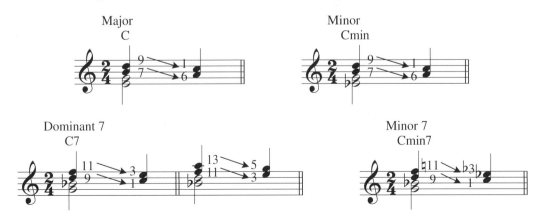

FIG. 9.16. Double Hi-Lo in C

Using "double Hi-Lo" wherever possible, figure 9.8 might be harmonized in the following manner:

FIG. 9.17. Double Hi-Lo Harmonization of Melody in Figure 9.8

ASSIGNMENT

1. Notate tensions of the six basic chord structures, starting on each of the following notes, similar to figure 9.1 and 9.7.

   C, F, B♭, E♭, A♭, D♭, G♭ (F♯), B, E, A, D, G

2. Starting on each of the above notes, notate the table showing harmonization of tensions. (See figures 9.4 and 9.5.)

3. Compose original melodies on each of the following chord progressions using "Hi-Lo" patterns only.

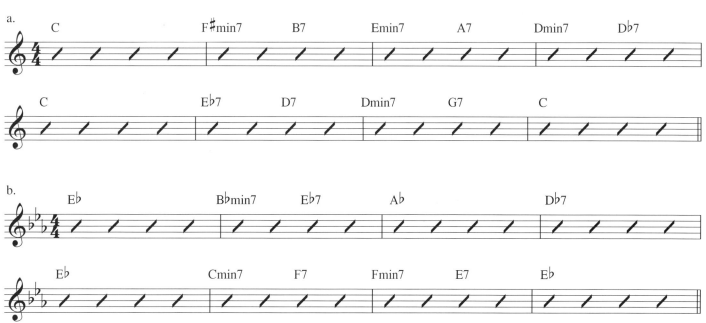

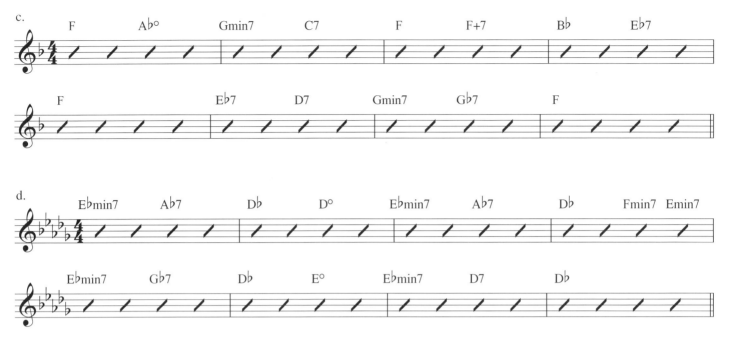

FIG. 9.18. Progressions for Problem 3

4. Again, using the list of root tones from problem No. 1, notate the table showing harmonization of "Hi-Lo." (See figures 9.10 and 9.11.)

5. In a similar manner, notate the table showing harmonization of tension-resolve using "double Hi-Lo." (See figures 9.15 and 9.16.)

6. Harmonize each of the melodies composed for problem 4. Use "double Hi-Lo" only where desired. (See figures 9.12 and 9.17.)

7. Analyze each of the melodies in figure 9.19, using the indicated coding. Remember that those notes that appear to be approach notes are still classified as approach notes. All principles of melodic analysis remain the same, except that those functions that were formerly indicated as non-chord, non-approach will now be named as tensions.

Chord Notes (low degree)	|
Tensions	by name
Hi-Lo	by name
Scalewise Approach Notes	s
Chromatic Approach Notes	ch
Double Chromatic Approach	d.c.
Delayed Resolve	d.r.

8. Complete a modern block harmonization of each of the given melodies. (See figures 9.18.)

FIG. 9.19. Practice Melodies

Variations of Hi-Lo, Altered Tensions

VARIATIONS OF HI-LO

In addition to the basic tension-resolve pattern that was discussed in lesson 9, there are several variations of Hi-Lo that may be effectively used.

Lo-Hi-Lo

FIG. 10.1. Lo-Hi-Lo

Following is a listing of all the possible forms of Lo-Hi-Lo on each of the six basic chord structures.

Major	6-7-6, 1-9-1
Minor	6-7-6, 1-9-1
Dominant 7	1-9-1, 3-11-3, 5-13-5
Minor 7	1-9-1, ♭3-11-♭3
Augmented 7	1-9-1, 3-♯11-3
Diminished 7	chord note-whole step above-chord note

FIG. 10.2. Lo-Hi-Lo

Figure 10.2 in musical notation would appear as follows:

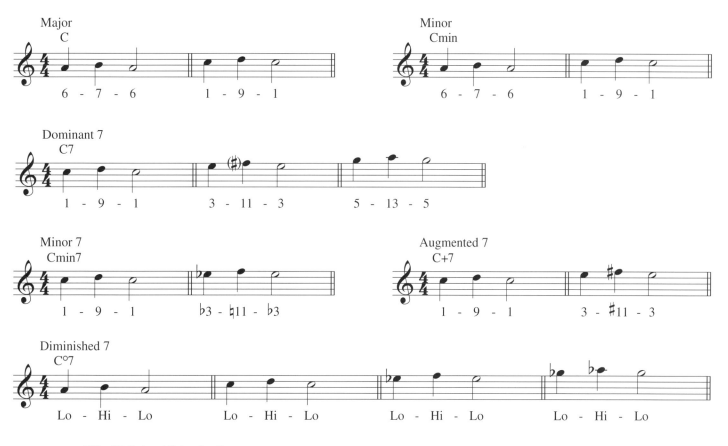

FIG. **10.3.** Lo-Hi-Lo in C

Hi-Chromatic-Lo

FIG. **10.4.** Hi-Chromatic-Lo

Following is an illustration showing all of the various possibilities for Hi-ch-Lo.

Major	7-ch-6, 9-ch-1
Minor	7-ch-6, 9-ch-1
Dominant 7	9-ch-1, ♯11-ch-3, 13-ch-5
Minor 7	9-ch-1, 11-ch-♭3
Augmented 7	9-ch-1, ♯11-ch-♭3
Diminished 7	Hi-ch-Lo

FIG. **10.5.** Hi-ch-Lo

NOTE: Hi-ch-Lo is not possible when moving from scale 11 to 3 on the dominant 7 chord.

Figure 10.5 in musical notation would appear as follows:

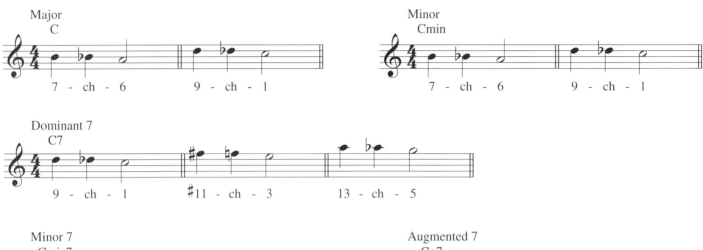

FIG. 10.6. Hi-ch-Lo in C

Lo-Hi-Chromatic-Lo

FIG. 10.7. Lo-Hi-Chromatic-Lo

The following chart includes all of the possible usages of Lo-Hi-ch-Lo.

Major	6-7-ch-6, 1-9-ch-1
Minor	6-7-ch-6, 1-9-ch-1
Dominant 7	1-9-ch-1, 3-♯11-ch-3, 5-13-ch-5
Minor 7	1-9-ch-1, ♭3-11-ch-♭3
Augmented 7	1-9-ch-1, 3-♯11-ch-3
Diminished 7	Lo-Hi-ch-Lo

FIG. 10.8. Lo-Hi–Chromatic-Lo

The preceding chart of Lo-Hi-ch-Lo would appear as follows in musical notation.

FIG. 10.9. Lo-Hi–Chromatic-Lo in C

(At this point it would be advisable to complete problems 1, 2, and 3 of the lesson assignment.)

An interesting melodic line may be composed by applying the preceding variations to a given chord progression. In the following example, only Hi-Lo and variations of Hi-Lo have been used.

FIG. 10.10. Melody with Hi-Lo and Variations

HARMONIZATION OF VARIATIONS OF HI-LO

1. Lo-Hi-Lo may be harmonized either of two ways.

   a. Sustain three lower voices while lead moves:

FIG. 10.11. Three Sustained Lower Voices

   b. Sustain two lower voices while two upper voices move in thirds (possible only where double Hi-Lo may be used; see lesson 9).

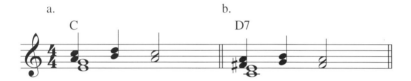

FIG. 10.12. Two Sustained Lower Voices, Upper Voices Move in Thirds

2. Hi-Chromatic-Lo may be harmonized as follows:

   a. Sustain three lower voices while lead moves:

FIG. 10.13. Three Sustained Lower Voices

   b. Sustain two lower voices while two upper voices move in thirds (possible only where double Hi-Lo may be used).

FIG. 10.14. Two Sustained Lower Voices, Upper Voices Move in Thirds

   c. Harmonize the "chromatic" as a chromatic approach note.

FIG. 10.15. Harmonized Chromatic

3. Lo-Hi-Chromatic-Lo may be harmonized by any of the following methods:

a. Sustain three lower voices while lead moves:

FIG. 10.16. Three Sustained Lower Voices

b. Sustain two lower voices while two upper voices move in thirds (only where double Hi-Lo could apply).

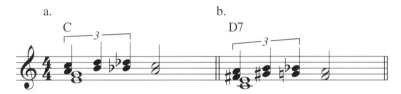

FIG. 10.17. Two Sustained Lower Voices, Upper Voices Move in Thirds

c. Harmonize the "chromatic" as a chromatic approach note:

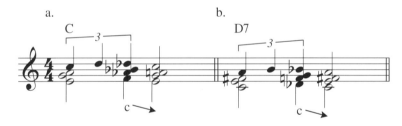

FIG. 10.18. Harmonized Chromatic

Using the preceding principles, the harmonization of figure 10.10 might appear as follows:

FIG. 10.19. Harmonization of Melody in Figure 10.10

ALTERED TENSIONS

In addition to the regular high-degree chord notes already discussed, certain "altered tensions" may be used in specific cases. They all occur with the dominant 7 chord and are:

FIG. 10.20. Altered Tensions of Dominant 7

The harmonization of these altered tensions would appear as follows:

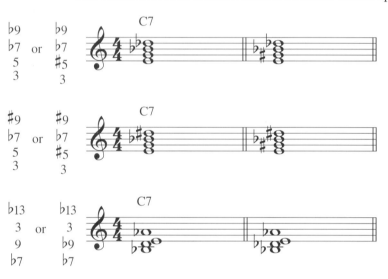

FIG. 10.21. Harmonized Altered Tensions

An effective form of Hi-Lo using altered tensions is ♯9 to ♭9 on the dominant 7 chord. The harmonization is as follows:

FIG. 10.22. Harmonized Hi-Lo Altered Tension

MELODIC ANALYSIS

This completes our classification of these melodic functions and patterns that may be effectively used and their respective harmonizations. Following is a complete listing with appropriate coding for melodic analysis.

Chord Notes	|
Scalewise Approach Notes	s
Chromatic Approach Notes	ch
Delayed Resolutions	d.r.
Double Chromatic Approaches	d.c.
Unresolved Tensions	by degree name
Hi-Lo and Variations of Hi-Lo	by degree name

It is important that you have a complete and thorough understanding of each of these melodic possibilities if you are to derive the maximum benefit from future lessons. Spend whatever time may be necessary in reviewing past lessons should there be any doubt whatsoever in your mind concerning their derivation or usage.

Here is an example of a melodic improvisation utilizing the above possibilities.

FIG. 10.23. Analyzed Melody

The modern block harmonization of figure 10.23 might appear as follows:

FIG. 10.24. Harmonization of Melody in Figure 10.23

Logically enough, these same possibilities may be employed in the melodic improvisation of a given melody. As in earlier discussions on improvisation, try to maintain the basic character of the original melody while using various devices to form an interesting melodic variation.

FIG. 10.25. Sample Melody and Improvisation

ASSIGNMENT

1. Notate all possible forms of Lo-Hi-Lo on each of the six basic chord structures, starting on each of the following notes: (See figures 10.2 and 10.3.)

   C, F, B♭, E♭, A♭, D♭, (F♯), B, E, A, D, G

2. Using the above list of starting notes, notate all forms of Hi-Chromatic-Lo. (See figures 10.5 and 10.6.)

3. Again, starting on each of the notes listed in problem 1, notate all possible forms of Lo-Hi-Chromatic-Lo. (See figures 10.8 and 10.9.)

4. Using the following chord progressions as a guide, compose original melodies based exclusively on Hi-Lo and its variations. (See figures 10.10.)

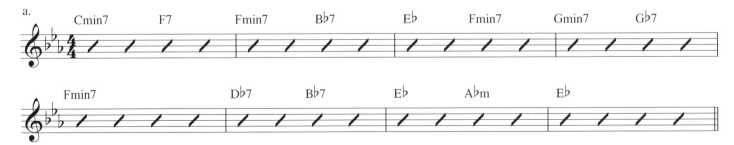

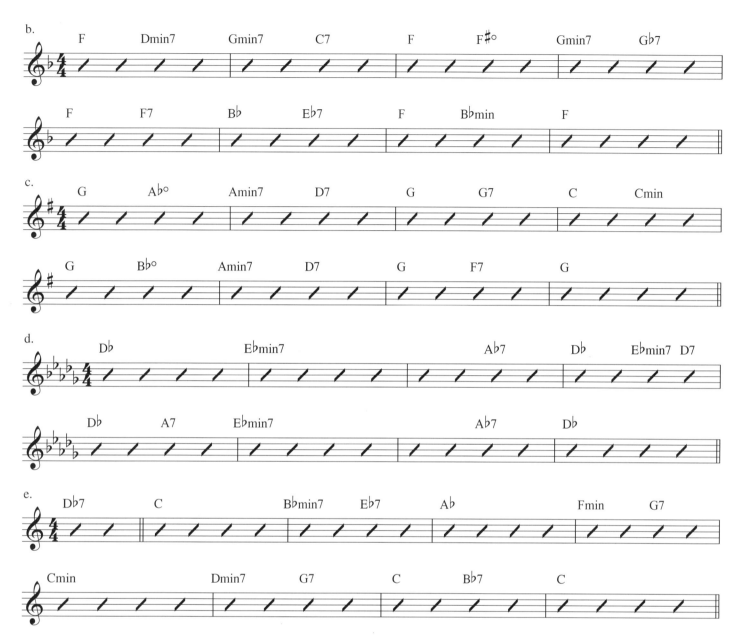

FIG. 10.26. Practice Progressions

5. Harmonize each of the melodies composed for problem 4 using any of the harmonization techniques discussed in this lesson. (See figure 10.19.)

6. Again using the chord progressions from problem 4 as a guide, compose original melodies utilizing all of the melodic variations catalogued in this lesson. Code each note as in figure 10.23.

7. Complete a modern block harmonization of each of the melodies composed in problem 6. (See figure 10.24.)

8. Again, utilizing these same melodic devices, write a melodic improvisation of any standard tune of your choice, being certain that the basic character of the original melody is retained. (See figure 10.25)

9. Write a modern block harmonization in open position of the melody resulting from problem 8.

The Reed Section

TRANSPOSITION

Various orchestral instruments require "transposition" from the original "concert" key.

B♭ Clarinet

Transpose up one whole step from the concert note.

This note:  played on the piano would sound the same as

this note:  played on clarinet.

This scale:

played on the piano, would sound the same as this scale:

played on the clarinet.

This same principle also applies to key relationships. For example, if the concert key were C, the clarinet part would be written in the key of D (one whole tone higher).

Here is a melodic line, first as it might appear in "concert" and then transposed for the B♭ clarinet.

FIG. 11.1. Melody Tranposed for B♭ Clarinet

E♭ Alto Sax

Transposes up a major sixth from the concert note.

This note:  played on the piano would sound the same as

this note: 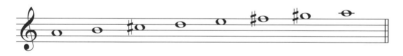 played on the alto sax.

This scale:

played on the piano, would sound the same as this scale:

played on the alto sax.

The transposed key relationship is also based on the interval of the major sixth, i.e., if the concert key were C, then the alto sax would be in the key of A.

Following is a melody, first in concert and then transposed for the E♭ alto sax.

FIG. 11.2. Melody Transposed for E♭ Alto Sax

B♭ Tenor Sax

Transposes up one whole step plus an octave from the concert note.

This note:  played on the piano would sound the same as

this note:  played on the tenor sax.

This scale:

played on the piano, would sound the same as this scale:

played on the tenor sax.

In finding the transposed key for the tenor sax, simply think "up one whole step," since the addition of the octave would not affect the key relationship in any way. If the concert key were E♭, the proper key for the tenor sax would be F.

Following is a melody, first as it might appear in concert and then transposed for the B♭ tenor sax.

FIG. 11.3. Melody Transposed for B♭ Tenor Sax

E♭ Baritone Sax

Transpose up a major sixth plus an octave from the concert note.

This note:  played on the piano would sound the same as

this note:  played on the baritone sax.

This scale:

played on the piano, would sound the same as this scale:

played on the baritone sax.

Since the extra octave does not affect the key relationship, simply figure a major sixth higher when determining the proper transposed key for the baritone sax.

If the concert key were C, the baritone sax part would be written in the key of A (the same as the alto sax).

To illustrate the foregoing, here is a melodic line, first in the concert key and then transposed for the E♭ baritone sax.

Concert

E♭ Baritone Sax

FIG. 11.4. Melody Transposed for E♭ Baritone Sax

NOTE: When transposing for the reed section, remember that the individual parts are always written in the treble clef, regardless of their appearance in the concert score.

RANGES

Naturally, there are certain limitations as to just how high and how low each instrument is capable of playing. The distance between the lowest note and the highest note is called the *range* of the instrument. The following illustration shows two sets of ranges for each instrument. The first is the "possible" range, i.e., the ordinary physical limitations of the instrument. The second is the "practical" range, i.e., the range that you may assume to be comfortable for any reasonably adequate instrumentalist. It is always wiser to confine your writing to the practical ranges. The extreme ranges should be used only where absolutely necessary or in cases where the arranger is familiar with the individual musician's facilities.

Remember that the best planned and most musically conceived score is of no practical value unless it can be comfortably played and interpreted by the instrumentalist. (Refer to "Range Chart" in figure 11.5.)

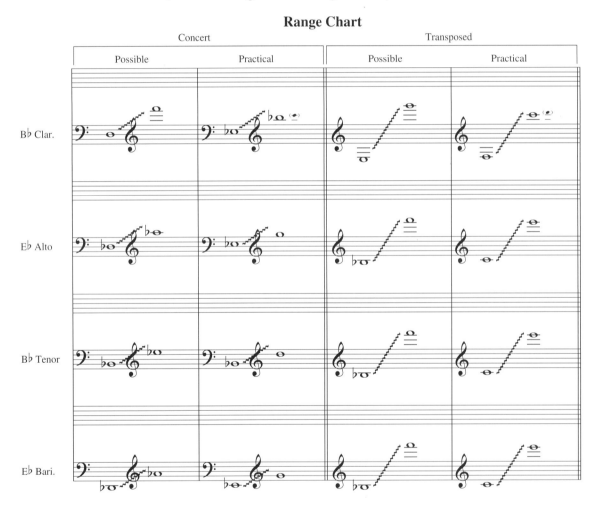

FIG. 11.5. Reed Section Ranges

VOICINGS

Although there are several different combinations of reed instruments that can be used in a four-part saxophone section, the most common is:

I   E♭ Alto Sax

II   E♭ Alto Sax

III B♭ Tenor Sax

IV   B♭ Tenor Sax

Let us assume that we have prepared a four-part block harmonization of a given melody in concert sketch form.

FIG. 11.6. Block Harmonization

To apply the aforementioned saxophone voicing to this block harmonization, transpose parts for the individual instruments as follows:

NOTE: Remember that the transposed key for E♭ instruments will be a major sixth higher than the concert key, and the transposition for the B♭ instruments will be one whole step higher than the concert key.

1. Transpose the top note all the way through for the first E♭ alto sax (see figure 11.6).

FIG. 11.7. Top Line Transposed for First Alto Sax

2. Transpose the second note (from the top) all the way through for the second E♭ alto sax (see figure 11.6).

FIG. 11.8. Second Line Transposed for Second Alto Sax

3. Transpose the third note (from the top) all the way through for the third voice, a B♭ tenor sax (see figure 11.6).

FIG. 11.9. Third Line Transposed for First Tenor Sax

4. Transpose the bottom note all the way through for the fourth instrument, the second B♭ tenor sax (see figure 11.6).

FIG. 11.10. Fourth Line Transposed for Second Tenor Sax

NOTE: In transposing individual parts, use enharmonic spelling wherever resulting notation seems more practical.

The resulting parts when played by the respective instrumentalists will produce the same sound as the original concert score, but with that distinctive quality that comes from the particular sax voicing used.

Another four-part sax voicing that is quite frequently used is as follows:

I   E♭ Alto Sax

II   B♭ Tenor Sax

III B♭ Tenor Sax

IV   E♭ Baritone Sax

This reed voicing is particularly effective when the four-part harmonization is converted to open position as discussed in lesson 3. As a reminder, here is the rule for producing open harmony:

To produce open harmony, drop the second voice (from the top) of any closed chord down one octave.

(Refer to lesson 3 for further detail regarding open harmony.)

Here is an example of a four-part harmonization in open position and the transposed parts written as they would appear using the above voicing.

FIG. 11.11. Melody, Open Voicing, and Saxophone Arrangement

Although the transposed parts have been written one above the other in the preceding example for the sake of convenience, it would be necessary to transpose the individual parts on separate sheets of manuscript if they were to be performed by individual instrumentalists.

Also, be sure to remember that it is essential that the parts be legibly and clearly written. The musicians will be able to give a better and more concentrated interpretation of the music if they are not forced to struggle to understand the notation.

EXPRESSION MARKS

An understanding of the proper usage of expression marks is vital to the arranger in transmitting his intentions and interpretation to the instrumentalist. Conversely, it is also essential that the instrumentalist understand and observe these expression marks carefully if the arranger's musical ideas are to be effectively performed.

Following is a reference chart of the most commonly used expression marks and their meaning.

Symbol	Name	Meaning
f	forte	loud
ff	fortissimo	very loud
fff	fortississimo	very, very loud
mf	mezzo forte	medium loud
p	piano	soft
pp	pianissimo	very soft
ppp	pianississimo	very, very soft
mp	mezzo piano	medium soft
	accent	attack sharply
	staccato	short
	tenuto	give full value
	drop	attack on pitch – slur off
	bend	lift, or upward slur off
	gliss.	lift or drop to given note
	slur	legato (play smoothly)
	fermata	hold
	crescendo	gradually louder
	decrescendo	gradually softer
tr ⌇⌇⌇	trill	trill
Rit.	ritard	gradually slower
D.C.	Da Capo	to the beginning
D.S.	Del segno	back to the Segno (𝄋)
𝄋	Segno	the sign
⊕	Coda	Coda
Fine	Fine	the end
D.S. al ⊕	D.S. al Coda	start back at the sign – play until Coda sign – then jump to Coda (play to Fine)
V. S.	volto subito	turn page quickly
8va	ottava alta	octave higher
8vb	ottava bassa	octave lower

FIG. 11.12. Expression Marks

In all future assignments, try to make use of expression marks in both score and parts to indicate your intentions as precisely as possible.

ASSIGNMENT

1. Write a four-part block harmonization of each of the following melodies.

FIG. 11.13. Practice Melodies

2. Using the following voicing, transpose the individual parts from the harmonizations in problem 1 for the reed section.

   I   E♭ Alto Sax

   II   E♭ Alto Sax

   III B♭ Tenor Sax

   IV   B♭ Tenor Sax

3. Write a four-part block harmonization of the following melodies in open position.

FIG. 11.14. Practice Melodies

4. Transpose the individual parts from the harmonizations in problem 3 using the following voicing:

   I   E♭ Alto Sax

   II   B♭ Tenor Sax

   III B♭ Tenor Sax

   IV   B♭ Tenor Sax

5. Write a four-part block harmonization of any standard tune of your choice and transpose parts as follows:

   I   B♭ Clarinet

   II   E♭ Alto Sax

   II   E♭ Alto Sax

   IV   B♭ Tenor Sax

Principles of Background Writing

The past several lessons have dealt primarily with various devices relating to block harmonization: the technique of concerting under voices to a moving melodic line in "block" fashion.

In this lesson, we concern ourselves with the principles of *background writing*: the technique of composing a supporting harmonic background to a separate melodic line.

The importance of a thorough understanding of the following material cannot be over-emphasized, since the ability to play or write effective background lines is essential.

The following outline will serve as a guide in composing a background to a given melody.

1. Using chord notes only, write a smooth melodic counter line based on the following principles:

    a. Where the melody moves, sustain the background; where the melody sustains, move the background.

FIG. 12.1. Complementary Rhythms

b. As in simple harmonic continuity, try to establish a smooth melodic connection between chords by sustaining, or moving chromatically or stepwise. However, leaps may occur freely while the chord remains the same.

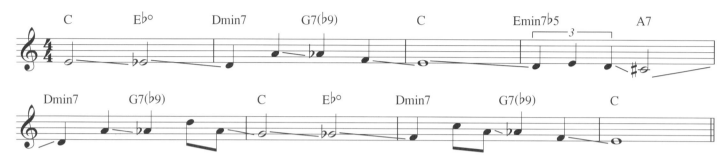

FIG. 12.2. Smooth Voicing and Leaps

c. Where melody and counter line attack at the same time, it is best (for the present) to keep the counter line at least a third, and not more than an octave, from the melody.

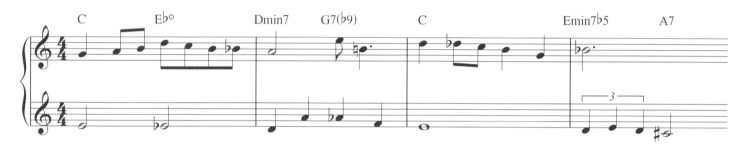

FIG. 12.3. Simultaneous Attacks

In figure 12.4, all points marked (X) would be considered to be bad.

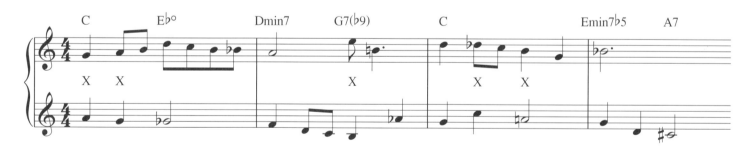

FIG. 12.4. Avoid These Cases

d. Where melody and counter line do not attack at the same time, they may cross freely.

FIG. 12.5. Asynchronous Attacks

2. After a line has been composed in accordance with the preceding principles, complete a block harmonization of this counter line.

FIG. 12.6. Given Melody with Harmonization

Here is another step-by-step illustration of the construction of a simple background to a given melody.

FIG. 12.7. Melody with Harmonization and Background

(At this point it would be advisable to complete problem 1 of the lesson assignment.)

Unresolved tensions may often be used effectively in composing the melodic counter line, which is to serve as the top voice of the background. The proper use of these tensions will create many new and interesting possibilities for smooth melodic connections between adjacent chords.

Here is an example of a background utilizing unresolved tensions in the top voice.

a.

FIG. 12.8. Background with Unresolved Tensions

Hi-lo and variations of Hi-Lo may also be used in background writing and will often serve to provide melodic interest where needed.

Note the effective use of Hi-Lo in the top voice of the following background.

a.

b.

FIG. 12.9. Background with Hi-Lo

To be certain that all of the foregoing is perfectly clear, here is another example of a background to a given melody employing not only low degree chord notes in the top voice, but unresolved tensions and variations of Hi-Lo as well.

a.

b.

FIG. 12.10. Melody with Backgrounds

As with regular block harmony, a closed background may be converted to open position by dropping the second voice down one octave. Here is the second example in figure 12.9 as it would appear in open position.

FIG. 12.11. Open Position

The subject of background writing will be continued in lesson 13 with a discussion of some additional techniques that are effective in writing good musical backgrounds, and a description of some of the many different styles of backgrounds that the arranger may be called upon to produce.

ASSIGNMENT

1. Write a background to each of the following melodies using the procedure described below:

    a. Compose a suitable top voice for the background using low-degree chord notes only.

    b. Complete the background by filling in the block harmonization of this top voice. (See figures 12.6 and 12.7.)

FIG. 12.12. Practice Melodies

2. Once again, write a background to each of the following melodies using the procedure described below:

   a. Compose a suitable top voice for the background using not only low-degree chord notes, but unresolved tensions and variations of hi-lo as well.

   b. Complete the background by filling in the block harmonization of this top voice. (See figure 12.10.)

c.

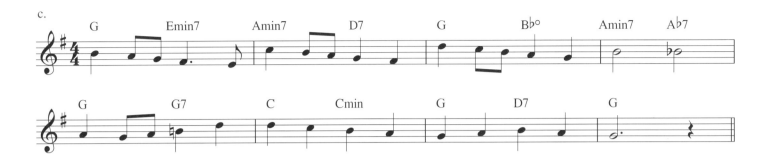

FIG. 12.13. Practice Melodies

3. Compose a background to each of the following melodies similar to problem 2, but harmonize each of the backgrounds in open position. In each case, compose the top voice first before completing the harmonization. (See figure 12.11.)

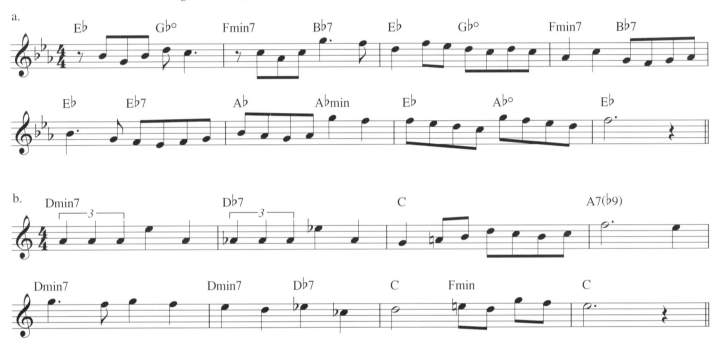

FIG. 12.14. Practice Melodies

4. Using the techniques described in this lesson, compose a background to any two standard tunes of your choice. Note: It would be advisable to select smooth ballads rather than swing type tunes, since many of the techniques relating to swing backgrounds will be covered in lesson 13.

5. Transpose parts from either one of the tunes in problem 4 as follows:

Solo Melody:		B♭ Clarinet
Background:	I	E♭ Alto Sax
	II	B♭ Tenor Sax
	III	B♭ Tenor Sax
	IV	E♭ Baritone Sax

Background Writing (Cont.)

APPROACH NOTES

All of the melodic approach techniques described in earlier lessons dealing with improvisation may also be used in background writing. These approach techniques are effective in creating added melodic interest in the background and will serve to provide many new and interesting possibilities for melodic variation.

In the following example, note the smooth melodic motion achieved through the occasional use of approach notes.

FIG. 13.1. Approach Notes

In order to avoid any melodic conflict, be sure to avoid attacking an approach note in the background at the same time that a chord note is being attacked in the melody. Figure 13.2 illustrates this point.

FIG. 13.2. Avoiding Simultaneous Attacks on Approach Notes

To further clarify this same principle, here is an example emphasizing the correct use of approach notes.

FIG. 13.3. Correct Use of Approach Notes

RESTS

The use of rests in the background will often serve to provide relief from the monotony that may result from a continuous sustained sound. There is no set rule as to when it is most advisable to use rests, but the following applications are frequently employed.

1. Rests may be used to subdivide the background into natural "phrases." These phrases are usually either two or four bars in length, and rests may be used in the background to emphasize the natural phrase division of the original melody.

FIG. 13.4. Rests as Phrase Endings

2. Rests may be used in creating a background made up of detached "figures." These figures are short melodic fragments that provide background interest during sustained or open portions of the melody. Following is an example of a background made up primarily of these fill-in figures.

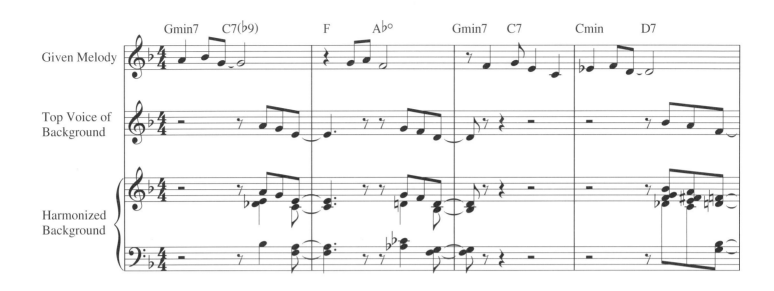

FIG. 13.5. Rests for Isolating Figures

SEQUENCE

Although the subject of sequence will be covered more thoroughly in future lessons, the principle of sequence in relation to background writing will be introduced at this time. Basically, sequence represents the reiteration of a previous phrase or figure in some recognizable form. Any variation of the original theme may be used, provided that a similarity between the two may be recognized by the listener.

Note the sequential relationship between the first two bars and the next two bars of the following example.

FIG. 13.6. Two-Bar Sequence

Following are several illustrations of sequential repetition:

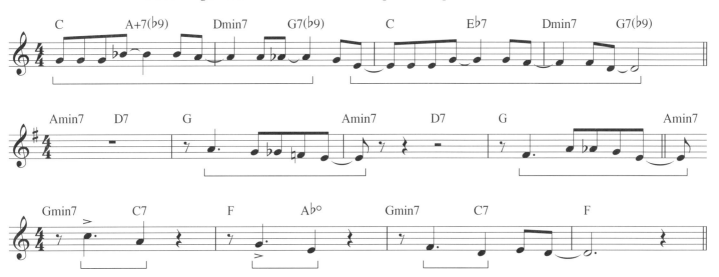

FIG. 13.7. Sequential Repetition

Figure 13.8 shows the use of "sequence" in composing the background to a given eight-bar melody.

FIG. 13.8. Sequence Example

SWING BACKGROUNDS

In composing the background to a swing type melody, the following principles should be observed:

1. Complement and emphasize the swing feeling of the melodic line through the use of anticipations and rhythmic figures in the background.

FIG. 13.9. Using Anticipation and Rhythmic Figures

2. Although sustained passages may occasionally be effectively used in a
    swing background, rely primarily on the rhythmic (and melodic) fill-in
    figures for added interest.

FIG. 13.10. Fill-In Figures

BACKGROUND STYLES

Probably the most important factor in background writing is the preservation of
the same feeling and mood in the background as has already been established by
the existing melody. If the melody is smooth and flowing in character, then the
background should complement it in similar manner. In a case where the melody has
a strong swing feeling, this same swing feeling should be present in the background.

Every tune must be treated as an individual problem and it is essential that you
exercise your own musical imagination and taste at all times. It is important that
you remember that the principles set forth in these lessons are designed to serve as
a guide rather than a restriction.

A careful study of the following examples should give you a more definite idea
of some of the many different styles of backgrounds that the arranger may be called
upon to produce.

FIG. 13.11. Smooth Ballad

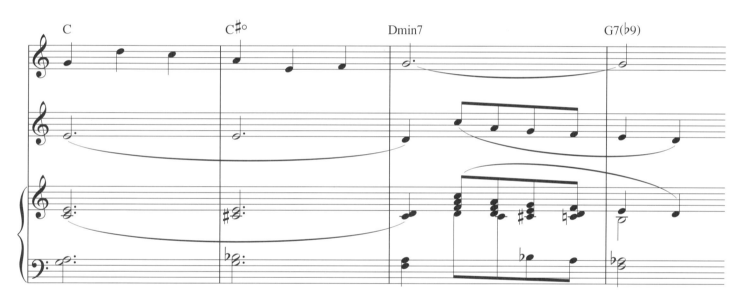

FIG. 13.12. Waltz

FIG. 13.13. Swing 1

FIG. 13.14. Swing 2

ASSIGNMENT

1. Making use of any or all of the techniques discussed thus far, write a musical background to each of the following melodies:

a.

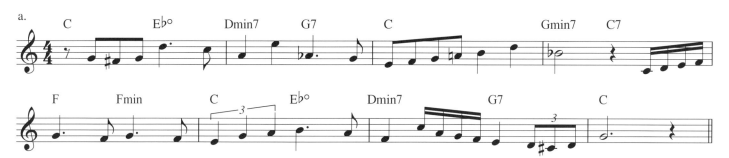

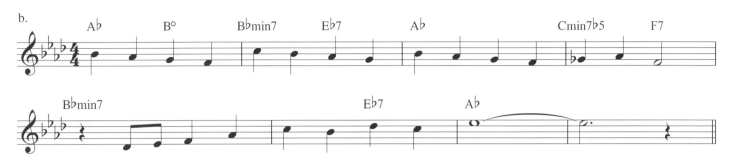

FIG. 13.15. Practice Melodies

2. Write a background to each of the following swing melodies, emphasizing the same swing feeling in the background.

FIG. 13.16. Practice Melodies

3. Compose a suitable background for each of the following melodies.

FIG. 13.17. Practice Melodies

4. Select a standard tune in each of the following styles and compose a background to each complete chorus.

    a.   Smooth ballad (fox trot)

    b.   Waltz

    c.   Swing

    d.   Beguine (or any tune utilizing the Latin-American beat)

5. Transpose parts from any one of the scores composed for problem 4 as follows:

Melody:		B♭ Clarinet
Background:	I	E♭ Alto Sax
	II	B♭ Tenor Sax
	III	B♭ Tenor Sax
	IV	E♭ Baritone Sax

LESSON 14

The Brass Section

TRANSPOSITION

B♭ Trumpet

Transpose up one whole step from the concert note.

This note: 🎼 played on the piano would sound the same as

this note: 🎼 played on trumpet.

This scale:

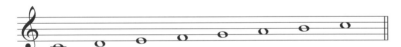

played on the piano, would sound the same as this scale:

played on the trumpet.

This same principle also applies to key relationship. If the concert key was C, the trumpet would have to be in the key of D (one whole tone higher). If the concert key was A♭, then the trumpet part would be written in the key of B♭.

Here is a melodic line, first as it might appear in concert and then as it would appear transposed for B♭ trumpet.

FIG. 14.1. Melody Tranposed for B♭ Trumpet

B♭ Trombone

NOTE: In contemporary usage, the "B♭" part of this instrument's name is no longer included. Just "trombone."

The B♭ trombone is a non-transposing instrument (in spite of its name). Each note is written exactly as it sounds.

This note: 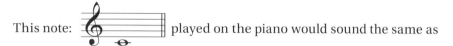 played on the piano would sound the same as

this note:  played on trombone.

This scale:

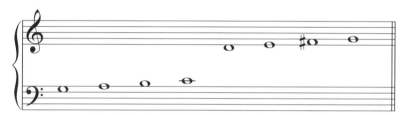

played on the piano, would sound the same as this scale:

played on the trombone.

Here is a melodic line, first as it might appear in concert and then as it is written for trombone. Regardless of where the notes appear on the concert score, trombone parts are always written in the bass clef.

NOTE: In contemporary usage, the tenor clef is also used for extended high trombone parts.

FIG. 14.2. Melody Tranposed for Trombone

RANGES

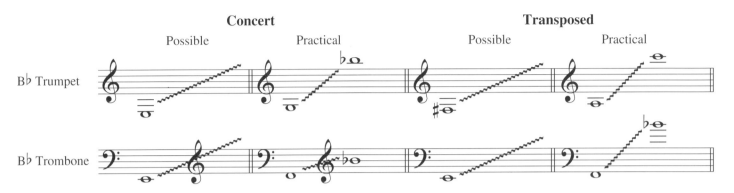

FIG. 14.3. Brass Section Ranges

No definite, possible upper limit may be set for the trumpet or trombone, the range being dependent solely upon the proficiency of the performer. In any event, it is advisable to adhere to the given practical range unless you are personally familiar with the capabilities of each member of the brass section.

VOICING

The four-part brass section normally consists of:

I   B♭ Trumpet

II   B♭ Trumpet

III B♭ Trumpet

I   B♭ Trombone

Let us assume that we have prepared a four-part block harmonization in concert sketch form:

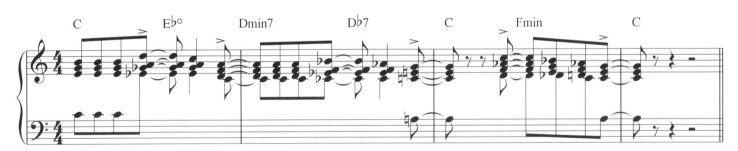

FIG. 14.4. Block Voicing

The individual parts transposed according to the above voicing would appear as follows:

I B♭ Trumpet

II B♭ Trumpet

III B♭ Trumpet

I Trombone

FIG. 14.5. Brass Section Harmonization (Transposed)

An alternate combination of instruments for a four-part brass section would be:

I   B♭ Trumpet

II   B♭ Trumpet

I   B♭ Trombone

II   B♭ Trombone

Here is an example of a four-part block harmonization in open position with parts transposed according to the voicing previously described.

FIG. 14.6. Block Harmonization

I B♭ Trumpet

II B♭ Trumpet

I B♭ Trombone

II B♭ Trombone

FIG. 14.7. Arranged for Brass

The five-part brass section would normally consist of:

I   B♭ Trumpet

II   B♭ Trumpet

III   B♭ Trumpet

I   B♭ Trombone

II   B♭ Trombone

FIVE-PART HARMONY

Since our work up to now has dealt exclusively with four-part writing, it is necessary at this time to discuss some of the techniques relating to five-part harmony if we are to work with a five-part brass section.

A simple five-part harmonization may be produced by doubling the original melody one octave below the lead.

a. Four-Part Harmony

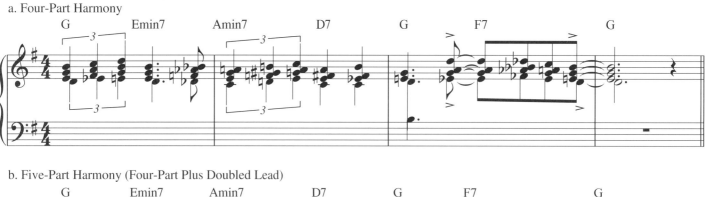

b. Five-Part Harmony (Four-Part Plus Doubled Lead)

FIG. 14.8. Block Harmonization

The transposed parts from the preceding example (figure 14.8b) would appear as follows:

FIG. 14.9. Arranged for Brass

A five-part harmony in open position may be achieved by doubling the original melody one octave below the lead and dropping the second voice down one octave as well.

FIG. 14.10. Closed and Open Position

BRASS SOLI

The principle of modern block harmonization as discussed in relation to the sax section may be effectively applied to the brass section as well. (See examples 14.4, 14.6, 14.8, and 14.10 of this lesson.) All of the previously mentioned approach techniques may be employed as well as all of the principles of improvisation covered in earlier lessons.

> **NOTE:** When scoring a block harmonization for brass (either closed or open), it is best to keep this lead trumpet above E♭ concert.

A brass soli (or background) scored any lower than this will result in a muddy and cumbersome sound.

When writing an improvised version of the original melody for the brass section, a rhythmic treatment is usually more effective than the smooth, flowing melodic style that is so effective in the sax section. Although it is true that brass may occasionally be written in this flowing "sax-like" style (just as saxes are occasionally used to provide a rhythmic, percussive "brass-like" effect), it is generally advisable to maintain some rhythmic interest in the brass soli.

FIG. 14.11. Given Melody and Improvisation

BRASS BACKGROUNDS

Smooth sustained melodic lines are often effective in brass backgrounds, particularly when applied to slow-tempo ballads, waltzes, etc. All principles of background writing as applied to the sax section still apply.

Following is an example of a brass background of this type.

FIG. 14.12. Brass Backgrounds

In the case of brass backgrounds to swing melodies, it is usually most effective to treat the brass section rhythmically rather than in the previously mentioned style. The use of rhythmic and/or percussive figures is especially effective.

FIG. 14.13. Brass Backgrounds in Swing

ASSIGNMENT

1. Write an improvised version of each of the following melodies that would be effective as the lead of a brass soli. In cases where the melody line goes too low, transpose to a higher, more suitable key.

FIG. 14.14. Practice Melodies

2. Score each of the improvised melodies in problem 1 for a five-part brass section (see examples 14.8b and 14.10b). Score at least two of the harmonizations in open position.

3. Transpose parts from each of the harmonizations in problem 2 for:

    I   B♭ Trumpet

    II   B♭ Trumpet

    III B♭ Trumpet

    I   B♭ Trombone

    II   B♭ Trombone

4. Using each of the following melodies as a guide, set up concert scores as shown below.

FIG. 14.15. Score Setup

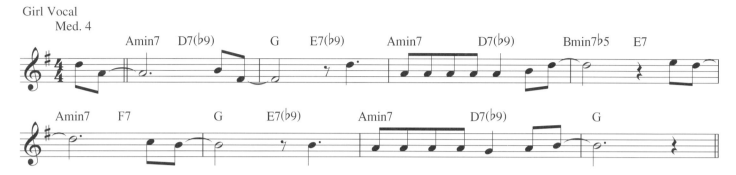

FIG. 14.16. Practice Melodies

It is important that you consider the character and feeling of each of the given melodies in deciding what type of background to use. Also, as you compose each background, try to imagine the sound of the given melody as played by the indicated instruments as well as the sound of the brass background. Use five-part harmony, either closed or open.

5. Using any standard tune of your choice, score a five-part brass soli in open position. Adapt the original melodic line in any way you choose and, if necessary, transpose the melody to a more suitable key before scoring the under voices.

6. Transpose parts from the score written for problem 5 for five brass (three trumpets and two trombones).

7. Using any swing tune of your choice, write a five-part brass background. Picture the original melody being played by a unison sax section. (**NOTE:** Set up the score as described in problem 4.)

8. Transpose parts from the above score for the regular five-part brass section.

Section Writing

MUTING

In the event that you are not familiar with the mutes commonly used in the brass section, following is a brief description of each:

1. **Straight mute.** Produces a thin metallic sound. Most effective in Latin-American style arrangements.

2. **Cup mute.** Best all-around mute in the brass section. Has soft metallic sound. Effective in both ballads and swing tunes.

3. **Harmon mute.** Has soft, distant quality. Effective in medium high to high register only. Most common in trumpet section.

4. **Brass hat.** Unlike other mutes, does not come into direct contact with the bell of the horn. Softens and mellows the sound, almost to a French horn timbre. Same effect often produced by blowing "in stand."

5. **Plunger.** Primarily used to produce "open/close" effect. (Listen to Glenn Miller records for excellent illustration of plunger work in the brass section.) Similar effect may be produced by using brass hat or cupping hand over bell, indicated as follows:

FIG. **15.1.** Plunger Mute Notation

NOTE: Avoid the use of mutes that are inserted directly into the bell (cup, straight, harmon, etc.) when writing in the low or medium-low register.

USE OF INNER-VOICE TENSIONS IN OPEN POSITION

Whenever you wish to achieve a tenser and more modern sound in the brass or sax soli, the following principle may be applied:

"Wherever possible, hi may be substituted for lo in the second voice (from the top) of any open voicing."

Following is a listing of the most practical and best sounding voicings employing the preceding principle:

Major Triad			Minor Triad				
3	5	5	3				
7	9	9	9				
5	6	7	6				
1	3	3	♭3				
Minor 7			**Dominant 7**				
5	♭7		1 or 9	5	♭7	♭9 or ♯9	♭13
9	♯11		13	9(♭9)	11	♭13	♭9
♭7	1		3	♭7	9	3	♭7
♭3	5		♭7	3	5	♭7	3

FIG. 15.2. Brass Voicings

The preceding in musical notation would appear as follows:

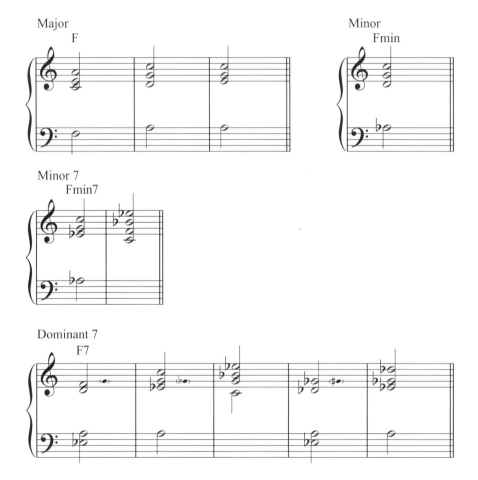

FIG. 15.3. Brass Voicings in C

These voicings are generally most effective when the lead voice lies between [musical notation] concert.

NOTE: The preceding voicings should be used only where the lead voice goes no lower than [musical notation] concert. With voicing marked *, the lead voice may be as low as [musical notation] concert.

Here is an example of a four-part sax soli in open position illustrating the usage of inner-voice tensions:

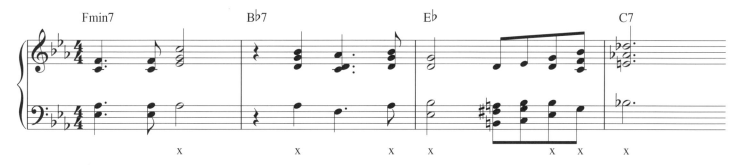

FIG. 15.4. Inner-Voice Tensions

It is important that you understand that these open voicings containing inner-voice tensions should be used only where good taste dictates. Do not feel that you must use inner-voice tensions every time the possibility exists. Rather, familiarize yourself with these sounds, and try to use them where you feel that their tense quality will be most effective.

In the following example, the given melody has been scored for a five-part brass soli (four-part with doubled lead) in open position. Voicings employing inner-voice tensions have been used where desired.

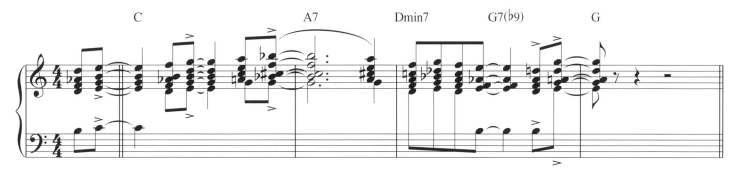

FIG. 15.5. Inner-Voice Tensions in Brass Soli

NOTE: Five-part brass soli in open position (second voice dropped) is most effective when the lead voice is between: [musical notation] concert.

THE FIVE-PART SAX SECTION

The most commonly used instrumentation in the five-part sax section is:

    I   E♭ Alto Sax

    II   E♭ Alto Sax

    III B♭ Tenor Sax

    IV B♭ Tenor Sax

    V   E♭ Baritone Sax

Either four-part, doubled lead in closed position, or four-part, doubled lead with second voice dropped, may be used with the above combination.

Following is an example of a five-part sax soli in open position (second voice dropped an octave).

FIG. 15.6. Five-Part Sax Soli

Another popular voicing for the five-part reed section is as follows:

    I   B♭ Clarinet

    II   E♭ Alto Sax

    III E♭ Alto Sax

    IV B♭ Tenor Sax

    V   B♭ Tenor Sax

This particular voicing is most effective in closed position and in a fairly high register, with the lead clarinet written no lower than   concert.

It is also interesting to note that this particular sound is commonly associated with the Glenn Miller band as well as those bands that have adopted the basic Miller style: Ralph Flanagan, Tex Beneke, etc.

Following is an example of a five-part sax soli scored for this instrumentation.

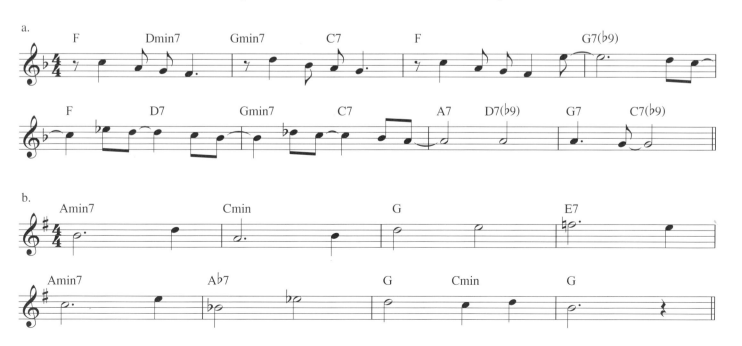

FIG. 15.7. Reeds with Clarinet Voicings

ASSIGNMENT

1. Notate the chart of open voicings utilizing inner-voice tensions in all keys. (See figure 15.3.)

2. Score each of the following melodies for a four-part sax section (alto, tenor, tenor, baritone). In each case, use open position, and utilize voicings containing inner-voice tensions where desired. (See figure 15.4.)

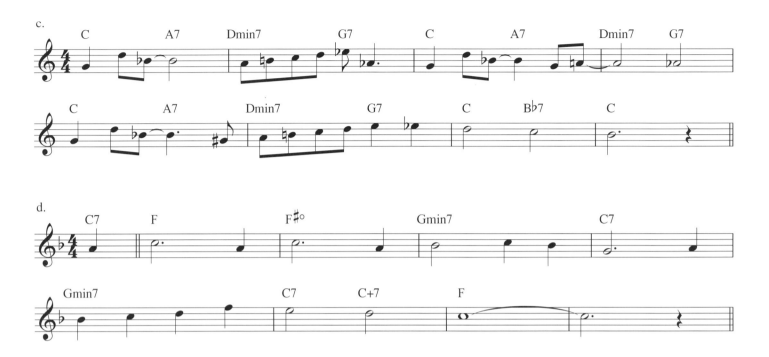

FIG. 15.8. Practice Melodies

3. Compose a melodic improvisation based on each of the following melodies so that it would be suitable as the lead of a brass soli. Where necessary, transpose to a higher key since each of the brass solis is to be scored in open position.

FIG. 15.9. Practice Melodies

4. Score each of the improvised melodies from problem 3 for a five-part brass soli in open position. Again, apply the principles of inner-voice tensions as described in this lesson.

5. Using melodies (a) and (b) from problem 2, set up a concert score as indicated in figure 15.10:

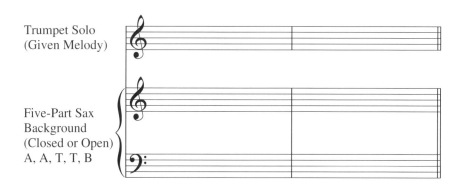

FIG. 15.10. Score Setup

6. Using melodies (c) and (d) from problem 2, set up a concert score as shown in figure 15.11:

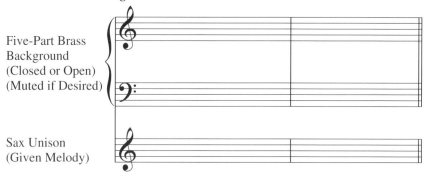

FIG. 15.11. Score Setup

7. Transpose any standard tune of your choice to a higher key so that the melodic line will be suitable as the lead voice of a five-part clarinet lead reed section. Feel free to alter the original melodic line in any way you see fit.

8. Score the transposed melody from problem 7 in closed position for:

    I   B♭ Clarinet

    II   E♭ Alto Sax

    III E♭ Alto Sax

    IV B♭ Tenor Sax

    V   B♭ Tenor Sax

Principles of Harmonic Progression I

At this point in the course, we come to one of the most essential and least understood subjects in modern music: modern chord progressions. In the next few lessons, you should achieve an excellent understanding of those principles that control present-day harmonic progressions.

You should ultimately be able to harmonize given melodic lines, correct "incorrect" chord changes, and reharmonize basic chord progressions to suit your personal taste.

TERMINOLOGY

For the purpose of this study, all chords will be named in relation to their position in the major-key scale.

Let us assume that we are composing (or analyzing) a chord progression in the key of C major:

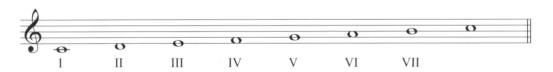

FIG. 16.1. Chord Degrees of C Major

Diatonic (i.e., using scale tones only) seventh chords built on the scale degrees will assume the following structures:

FIG. 16.2. Diatonic Seventh Chords of C Major

Non-diatonic chords may be indicated in a similar manner. In the key of C major:

- ♭VIMaj7   A♭Maj7
- ♭IIImin7   E♭min7
- ♯1°   C♯°
- etc.

FIG. 16.3. Non-Diatonic Chords in the Key of C Major

Wherever a dominant seventh structure is used as a V7 chord (i.e., moves to another chord a fifth below), we will name the V7 in relation to its forward tendency. For example, C7 to F in the key of C would not be analyzed as I7 to IV, but rather, as <u>V7 of IV</u> to IV. The symbol ⟶ will be used to indicate the resolution of any V7 chord, i.e., **V7 of IV – IV**.

Some additional examples of this point follow:

Key of C Major

B7	to	Emin	V7 of III	to	IIImin
D7	to	G7	V7 of V	to	V7
A7	to	Dmin7	V7 of II	to	IImin7

etc.

FIG. 16.4. Examples of Secondary Dominants

Following is an example of a simple chord progression outlined in the manner described and its appearance when related to a given key.

	I	VImin7	IImin7	V7	I	V7 of IV	IV	IVmin	I	♭VI7	I
Key of C:	C	Amin7	Dmin7	G7	C	C7	F	Fmin	C	A♭7	C
Key of E♭:	E♭	Cmin7	Fmin7	B♭7	E♭	E♭7	A♭	A♭min	E♭	C♭7	E♭
Key of A:	A	F♯min7	Bmin7	E7	A	A7	D	Dmin	A	F7	A

FIG. 16.5. Examples of Chord Progressions with V7 of IV

PRINCIPLES OF MODERN HARMONY

1. Any I chord may be preceded by its V7 (a dominant cadence).

This usually occurs over the bar line.

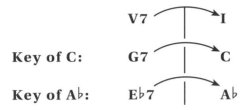

FIG. 16.6. Dominant Cadence

2. Any V7 may be preceded by the V7 of V (extension of the dominant cadence).
   Again, this usually (but not always) occurs over the bar line.

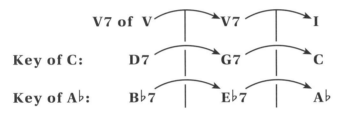

FIG. 16.7. Extension of Dominant Cadence

This same principle may be further extended as follows:

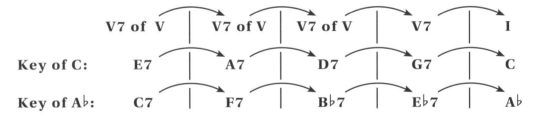

FIG. 16.8. Further Extension of Dominant Cadence

3. Any V7 may be immediately preceded by the related IImin7. This usually
   occurs within the bar.

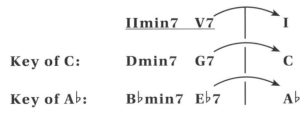

FIG. 16.9. Preceding V7 with IImi7

The use of the above does not affect the V7 of V relationship as established in
principle 2.

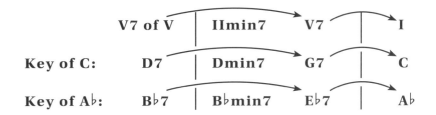

FIG. 16.10. V7 of V and IIMin7

Using as a basis the progression:

FIG. 16.11. Progression with V7 of V

...this same principle may be developed as follows:

Key of C:

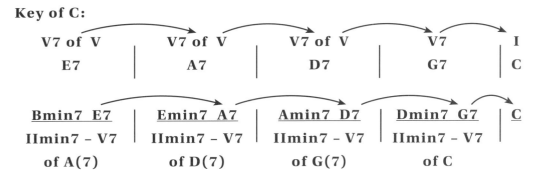

FIG. 16.12. V7 of V Progression in Key of C

Leading into the key of A, the preceding progression would appear as follows:

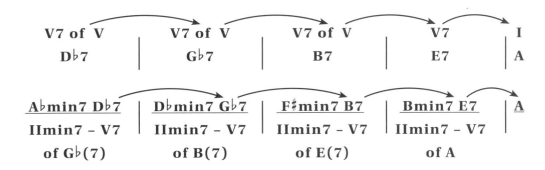

FIG. 16.13. IImin7 to V7 Progressions in the Key of A

NOTE: Changing from sharps to flats is permissible, but always over the bar line rather than within the bar.

4. Any IImin may be preceded by the V7 of II. This usually occurs over the
    bar line.

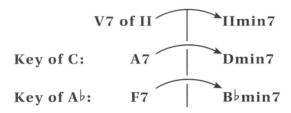

FIG. 16.14. Preceding IImin with V7 of II

A further development of this principle when combined with those preceding
would lead to the following result:

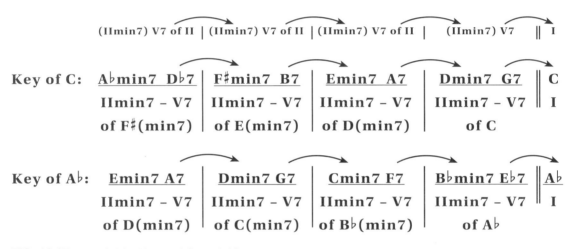

FIG. 16.15. V7 of II in Keys of C and A♭

The preceding progressions may be more easily understood by realizing that
any V7 chord, whether it be V7, V7 of V, V7 of II, etc., may be preceded by the related
IImin7, i.e... IImin7 to V7 of...

Since the IImin7 V7 pattern plays such an important part in modern chord
progression, it would be advisable at this point to familiarize yourself with this
pattern in all keys.

IImin7	V7	Major, Minor, Dominant7, or Minor 7
Dmin7	G7	C
E♭min7	A♭7	D♭
Emin7	A7	D
Fmin7	B♭7	E
Gmin7	C7	F
A♭min7	D♭7	G♭
Amin7	D7	G
B♭min7	E♭7	A♭
Bmin7	E7	A
Cmin7	F7	B♭
C♯min7	F♯7	B

FIG. **16.16.** II V I in All Keys

All of the principles discussed thus far may be intermingled in a harmonic progression with the forward tendency in each bar consisting of either the V7 of V or the V7 of II.

	(IIm7) V7 of V	(IIm7) V7 of II	(IIm7) V7 of V	(IIm7) V7	I
Key of C:	**F♯min7 B7**	**Bmin7 E7**	**Amin7 D7**	**Dmin7 G7**	**C**
	IImin7 – V7	**IImin7 – V7**	**IImin7 – V7**	**IImin7 – V7**	**I**
	of E(7)	**of A(min7)**	**of G(7)**	**of C**	

FIG. **16.17.** V7 of V, V7 of II Forward Tendency

Following is another example of the result obtained by combining the V7 of V and the V7 of II in a chord progression.

	(IImin7) V7 of V	(IImin7) V7 of II	(IImin7) V7 of II	(IImin7) V7	I
Key of C:	**C♯min7 F♯7**	**F♯min7 B7**	**Emin7 A7**	**Dmin7 G7**	**C**
	IImin7 – V7	**IImin7 – V7**	**IImin7 – V7**	**IImin7 – V7**	**I**
	of B(7)	**of E(min7)**	**of D(min7)**	**of C**	

FIG. **16.18.** Combining V7 of V, V7 of II

(At this point it would be advisable to complete problem 1 of the lesson assignment.)

CHORD PATTERNS

A detailed analysis of the chord changes to many hundreds of popular and standard tunes has revealed the existence of certain definite harmonic patterns. Since these patterns occur so frequently, it is certainly advantageous to be able to identify them and apply them in all keys.

The value of a thorough knowledge of these patterns cannot be stressed too strongly. Sufficient familiarity with them will enable you to transpose or memorize the chord changes to any tune virtually at sight. Further, since you are dealing with those very same elements which go to make up the chord changes to most tunes, you should have no difficulty whatsoever in composing original chord progressions in the same style.

Pattern #1

	I	VImin7	IImin7	V7	
Key of C:	C	Amin7	Dmin7	G7	‖
Key of A♭:	A♭	Fmin7	B♭min7	E♭7	‖

Pattern #2

	I	♯I°	IImin7	V7
Key of C:	C	C♯°	Dmin7	G7
Key of A♭:	A♭	A°	B♭min7	E♭7

Pattern #3

	I	♭III°	IImin7	V7	
Key of C:	C	E♭°	Dmin7	G7	‖
Key of A♭:	A♭	B°	B♭min7	E♭7	‖

Pattern #4

	V7 of V	IImin7	V7	I
Key of C:	D7	Dmin7	G7	C
Key of A♭:	A♭ B♭7	B♭min7	E♭7	A♭

Pattern #5

	V7 of II(♭9)	IImin7	V7	I	
Key of C:	A7(♭9)	Dmin7	G7	C	‖
Key of A♭:	F7(♭9)	B♭min7	E♭7	A♭	‖

Pattern #6

	I	V7 of IV	IV	IVmin	I
Key of C:	C	C7	F	Fmin	C
Key of A♭:	A♭	A♭7	D♭	D♭min	A♭

FIG. 16.19. Chord Patterns

Using only techniques that have been discussed up to this point, it is possible to create an infinite number of musical and practical (though still very simple) chord progressions.

One further principle, however, must be known and applied: *Anything may follow the I chord.*

Following are some logical eight-bar chord progressions along with an explanation of the function of each chord. Only materials contained in this lesson have been used.

(*Anything may follow the I chord.)

FIG. 16.20. Eight-Bar Chord Progressions

NOTE: It is possible in the course of a progression to establish a key other than the one indicated in the key signature. The following chord changes to effectively illustrate this point.

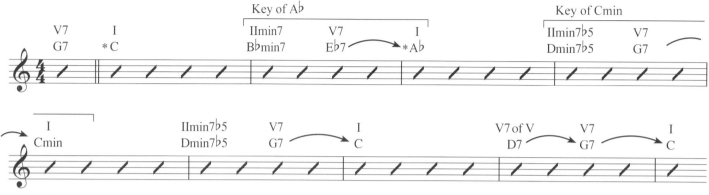

(*Anything may follow the I chord.)

FIG. 16.21. Progression with Key Change

ASSIGNMENT

1. Work out each of the following chord progressions in every key. (In each case, work back from the I chord.)

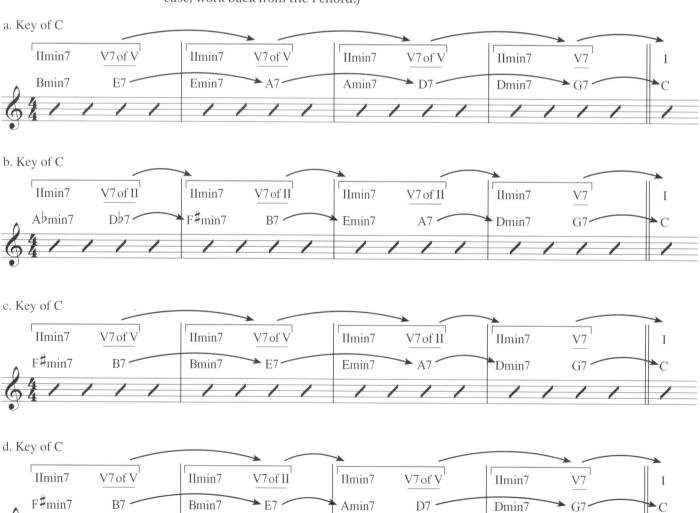

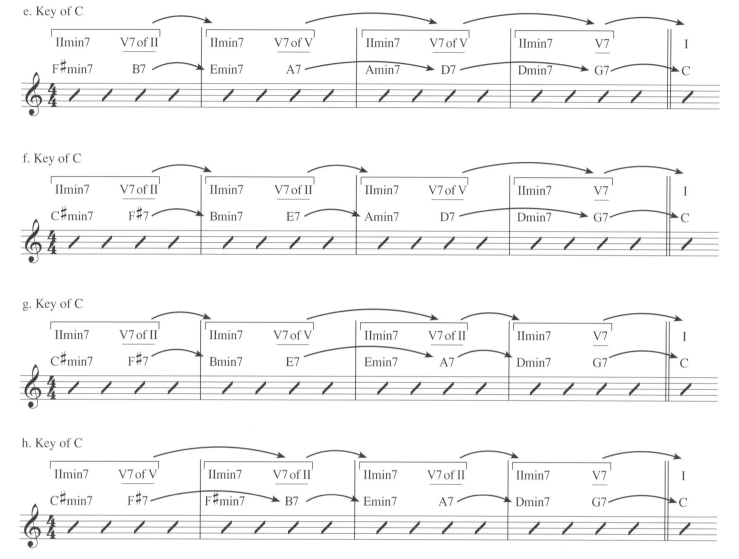

FIG. 16.22. Practice Progressions

2. Work out patterns 1, 2, 3, 4, 5, and 6 in all keys.

3. Compose three eight-bar progressions in every key using only those materials contained in this lesson. Explain the function of each chord used as in figure 16.20.

4. Using any and all of the melodic techniques covered in the preceding lessons (approach notes, tensions, tension-resolve, delayed resolution, etc.) compose original melodic lines to any twelve of the progressions resulting from problem 3.

5. Using any one of the original melodies composed for problem 4, set up a concert score as indicated below.

FIG. 16.23. Score Setup 1 for Arranging Problem 4

6. Again, using any other original melody from problem 4, set up a concert score as described below.

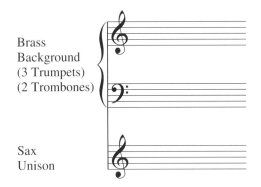

FIG. 16.24. Score Setup 2 for Arranging Problem 4

Principles of Harmonic Progression II

SUBSTITUTE CHORDS

Substitute chords of one type or another may often be effectively employed where a more "tense" or more modern sound is desired. Needless to say, they should not be used indiscriminately, but rather to achieve a specific effect at a specific point in the harmonic progression.

Following is a description of the most commonly used substitutions.

1. Substitute for the I chord. The IIImin7 may be used as a substitute for the major I chord.

The relationship of the IIImin7 to the I chord may be noted in the following illustration.

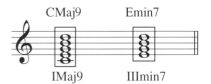

FIG. 17.1. IMaj9 and IIImin7

Observe the application of this principle to the example:

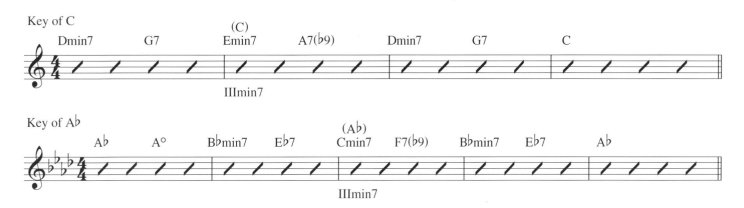

FIG. 17.2. Substituting IIImin7 for I

NOTE: This substitution is effective only in the middle of a progression and should not be used where the I chord is intended to signify a final cadence.

It should also be noted that it is almost always followed by some form of the V7 of II.

2. Substitute for the IVmin chord. The ♭VII7 may be used as a substitute for the IVmin.

Again, the derivation of this substitution may be noted in the following illustration:

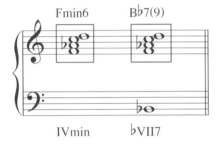

FIG. 17.3. IVmin and ♭VII7

Application of this principle might appear as follows:

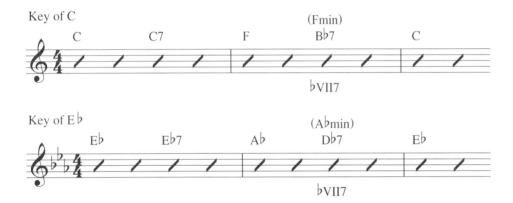

FIG. 17.4. Substituting ♭VII7 for IVmin

3. Substitute for the "V7" chord. The ♭II7 may be used as a substitute for the V7 chord.

Notice that the third and the seventh degree (which establish the chord as a dominant 7 structure) are the same in each case.

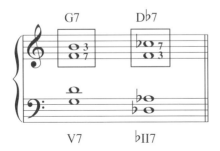

FIG. 17.5. V7 and ♭II7

In the following examples are illustrated some of the many, many applications of this principle.

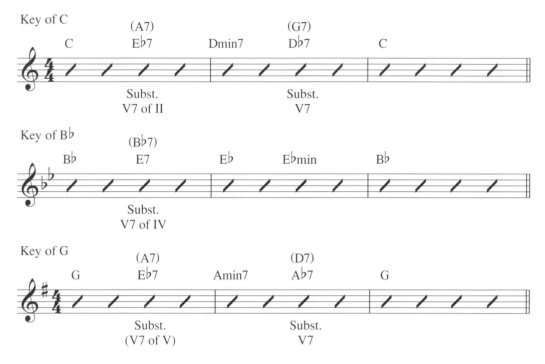

FIG. 17.6. Substituting ♭II7 for V7

Following is a reference chart illustrating all of the substitute chords described in this lesson.

(a) Substitute I (IIImin7)		(b) Substitute IVmin (♭VII7)		(c) Substitute V7 (♭II7)	
Original	Substitute	Original	Substitute	Original	Substitute
C	Emin7	Fmin6	B♭7	G7	D♭7
D♭	Fmin7	G♭min6	C♭7	A♭7	D7
D	F♯min7	Gmin6	C7	A7	E♭7
E♭	Gmin7	A♭min6	D♭7	B♭7	E7
E	G♯min7	Amin6	D7	B7	F7
F	Amin7	B♭min6	E♭7	C7	G♭7
F♯	A♯min7	Bmin6	E7	D♭7	G7
G♭	B♭min7	Cmin6	F7	D7	A♭7
G	Bmin7	D♭min6	G♭7	E♭7	A7
A♭	Cmin7	Dmin6	G7	E7	B♭7
A	C♯min7	E♭min6	A♭7	F7	B7
B♭	Dmin7	Emin6	A7	G♭7	C7
B	D♯min7				

FIG. 17.7. Common Substitute Chords

By preceding the V7 chord with either the original IImin7 or the related IImin7, the following variations are possible:

Key of C:	Dmin7	G7	C (or G♭)
	Dmin7	D♭7	C (or G♭)
	A♭min7	D♭7	C (or G♭)
	A♭min7	G7	C (or G♭)

Note the varied possibilities for a four-chord cadence utilizing this technique.

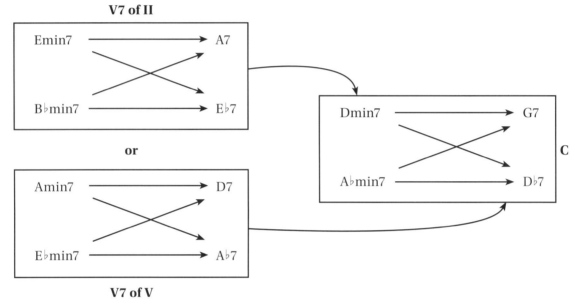

FIG. 17.8. Variations of a Four-Chord Cadence

Any combination of the above may be used providing that the forward motion is maintained.

Following are some examples of chord progressions employing all of the substitutions described in this lesson.

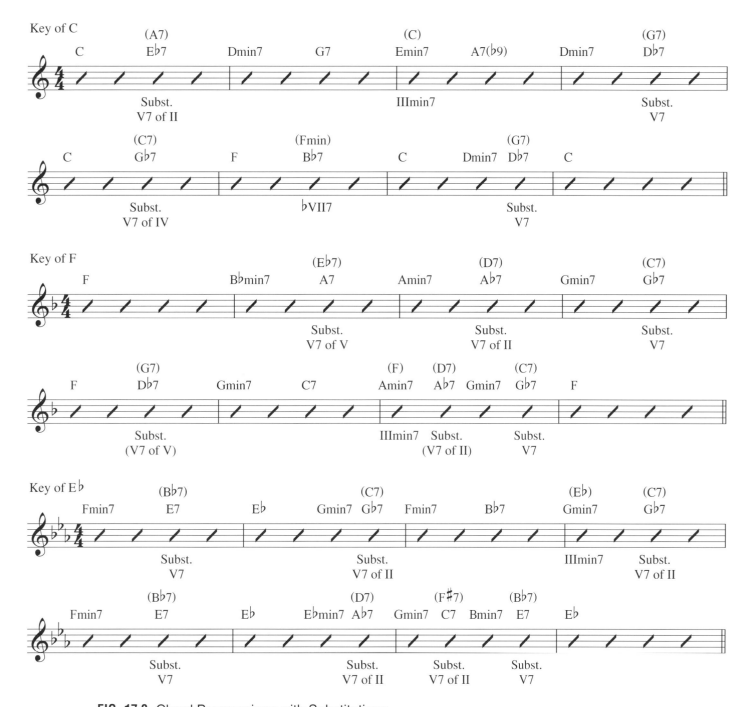

FIG. 17.9. Chord Progressions with Substitutions

This principle of the substitute dominant may be more easily mastered by remembering the following:

- V7 resolves down a fifth.

- Substitute V7(♭II7) resolves down a half step.

VARIATIONS OF THE BASIC I VI II V PATTERN

The pattern "I VImin7 IImin7 V7" is undoubtedly one of the most commonly used in popular harmonic progression. Following is a listing of the most practical variations of this basic chord pattern. Each of the variations has a slightly different character and a thorough familiarity with the sound of each will be important to you in deciding just which one to use in a given situation.

a.	I		VImin7		IImin7	**V7
b.	I		♭IIIº		IImin7	**V7
c.	I		♯Iº		IImin7	**V7
d.	I		V7 of V		IImin7	**V7
e.	I		sub. V7 of V		IImin7	**V7
f.	I		V7 of II(♭9)		IImin7	**V7
g.	I		sub. V7 of II		IImin7	**V7
h.	I	*IImin7	IIImin7	♭IIIº	IImin7	**V7
i.	I	*IImin7	IIImin7	♭IIImin7	IImin7	**V7
j.	I	*IImin7	IIImin7	V7 of II(♭9)	IImin7	**V7
k.	I	*IImin7	IIImin7	subV7 of II	IImin7	**V7
(Special Case) l.	I		V7 of ♭VI		♭VIMaj7	sub.V7

*IImin7 may be omitted in each case

**Substitute V7 may be used where desired

FIG. 17.10. Variations of I VI II V

The preceding list of variations would appear as follows in the key of C.

a.	C		Amin7		Dmin7	G7
b.	C		E♭IIIº		Dmin7	G7
c.	C		C♯º		Dmin7	G7
d.	C		D7		Dmin7	G7
e.	C		A♭7		Dmin7	G7
f.	C		A♭7(♭9)		Dmin7	G7
g.	C		E♭7		Dmin7	G7
h.	C	Dmin7	Emin7	E♭º	Dmin7	G7
i.	C	Dmin7	Emin7	E♭min7	Dmin7	G7
j.	C	Dmin7	Emin7	A7(♭9)	Dmin7	G7
k.	C	*IImin7	Emin7	E♭7	Dmin7	G7
l.	C		E♭7		A♭Maj7	D♭7

FIG. 17.11. I VI II V Variations in the Key of C

More complex variations may be produced in patterns d., e., f., g., and l. by preceding the V7 chord in the first bar with the related IImin7.

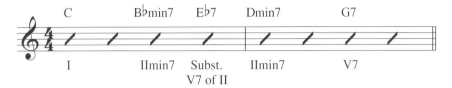

FIG. 17.12. Preceding V7 with IImin7

CADENCE

The term "cadence" is used to indicate the arrival of the harmonic progression at a point of rest (usually on the I chord).

The strength or finality of the cadence is determined by the character of the chords leading toward this point of resolution. Generally speaking, cadential motion may be classified according to the following forms:

1. Subdominant Cadence

2. Subdominant Minor Cadence

3. Dominant Cadence

The *subdominant cadence* is the least final and most subtle in feeling of the three possible forms. It may be expressed in any of the following ways:

IV	to	I
IImin7	to	I
*IV7	to	I

*Special Case: Used primarily in blues, or to establish a "blues" feeling.

FIG. 17.13. Subdominant Cadences

Key of C:

F	to	C
Dmin7	to	C
F7	to	C

The *subdominant minor cadence* has a stronger tendency toward resolution than the subdominant, and is somewhat more modern in feeling. The subdominant minor cadence may be represented as:

IVmin	to	I
IImin7♭5	to	I
♭VII7	to	I

FIG. 17.14. Subdominant Minor Cadence

Possibilities for subdominant minor cadence would appear as follows:

Key of C:

Fmin	to	C
Dmin7♭5	to	C
B♭7	to	C

FIG. 17.15. Subdominant Minor Cadences in C

The *dominant cadence,* which is the strongest and most final in feeling, is the familiar form most commonly associated with the term "cadence."

A dominant cadence may be achieved through:

V7	to	I
♭II7	to	I

Key of C:

G7	to	C
D♭7	to	C

FIG. 17.16. Dominant Cadence

There are also several less commonly used forms of subdominant and subdominant minor cadences that bear mentioning at this time. Although not usually found in basic chord progressions, these variations may often be effectively applied in reharmonization or in the composition of original chord progressions.

Subdominant:

VII7	to	I

Key of C:

B7	to	C

FIG. 17.17. Subdominant Cadences (Less commonly used forms)

Subdominant minor:

♭VIMaj7	to	I
♭VI7	to	I
♭IIMaj7	to	I

Key of C:

A♭Maj7	to	C
A♭7	to	C
D♭Maj7	to	C

FIG. 17.18. Subdominant Minor Cadences (Less commonly used forms)

Different cadential tendencies may be used in combination in leading toward the I chord. Any combination may be used providing that forward motion is maintained by using these tendencies in order of their relative strength. This order may be described as follows:

Subdominant ⟶ Subdominant Minor ⟶ Dominant ⟶ Tonic

Following is a listing of all the possible cadential forms that could result from the above outline:

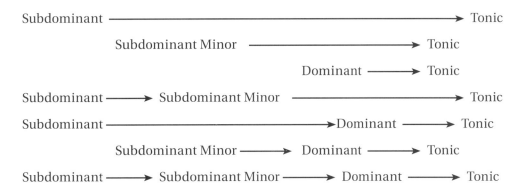

FIG. 17.19. Cadential Functional Variations

To illustrate further, let us assume that we have selected as our cadential form:

Subdominant ⟶ Subdominant Minor ⟶ Tonic

Referring to the possibilities for each tendency as described earlier in this lesson, we find that this particular cadence may assume the following appearance:

IV	IVmin	I
IImin7	IImin7♭5	I
IImin7	♭VII7	I
IV	♭VII7	I
Etc., etc.		

FIG. 17.20. Cadence Variations

Let us assume that we have selected as our cadence form:

Subdominant ⟶ Subdominant Minor ⟶ Dominant ⟶ Tonic

Here are some of the possible variations that might result:

IImin7	IImin7♭5	V7	I
IV	IImin7♭5	V7	I
IV	♭VII7	V7	IIImin7
IImin7	♭VII7	♭II7	I
Etc., etc.			

FIG. 17.21. Cadence Variations

It should by now be apparent to you that literally hundreds of varied and interesting cadential progressions may be evolved through the use of this system. Most of these forms are currently in common use in the basic chord changes to standard and popular tunes; all may be effectively used in reharmonization or in the composition of original chord progressions.

Remember, however, the forward motion must be maintained.

ASSIGNMENT

1. (a) Analyze each of the following chord progressions according to the techniques described in lesson 16.

    (b) Reharmonize each progression by employing substitute chords as described in this lesson.

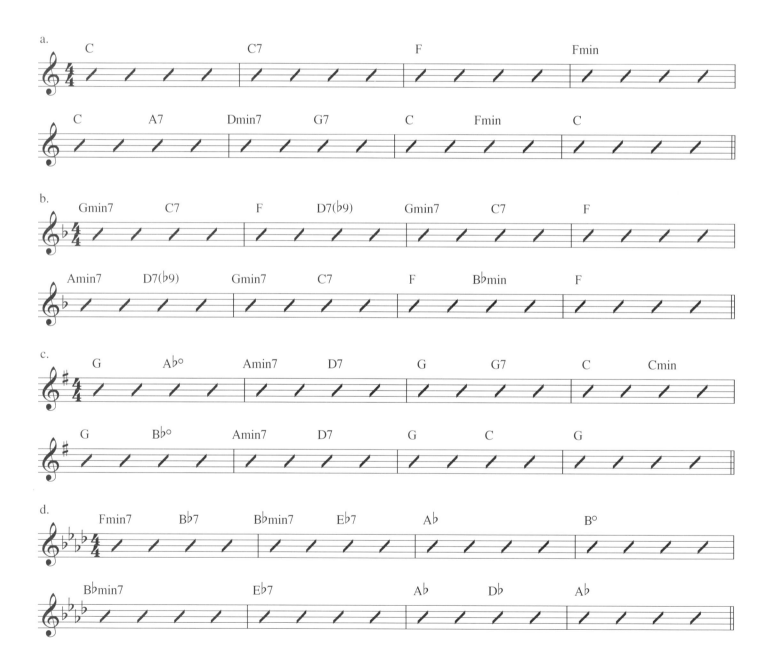

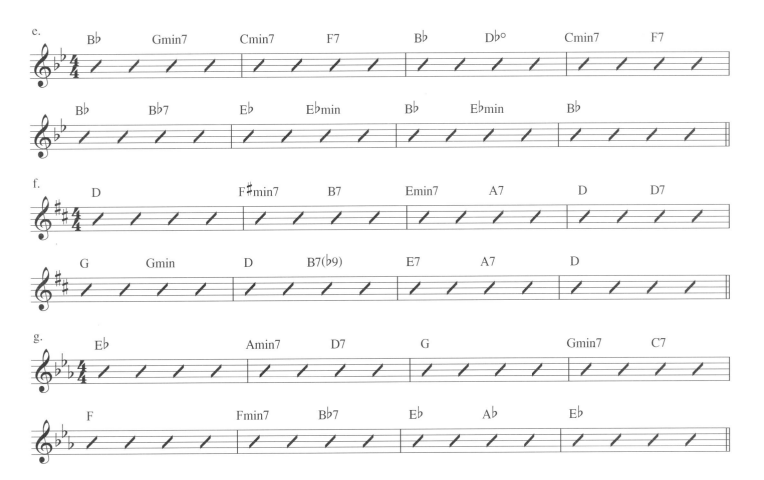

FIG. 17.22. Practice Progressions

2. Work out all variations of the basic I, VI, II, V, pattern in all keys.

3. Work out all possibilities for subdominant cadence in all keys.

4. Work out all possibilities for subdominant minor cadence in all keys.

5. Work out all possibilities for dominant cadence in all keys.

6. Working in all keys, show one possibility for each of the cadence forms listed on page 187.

7. Using all of the materials contained in lessons 16 and 17, compose two eight-bar progressions in every key.

8. Using any standard tune of your choice as a guide, work out the following:

    a. Transpose to a key suitable for a female vocalist.

FIG. 17.23. Female Vocalist Range

    b. Score a suitable background (to the vocal lead) for a five-sax section (A, A, T, T, B) using closed and/or open position.

Principles of Harmonic Progression III

REPETITION OF THE IImin7 V7

In the course of a harmonic progression, the IImin7–V7 of the key may be repeated without affecting the basic forward motion of the progression.

Key of C

IImin7	V7		IImin7	V7		I	
Dmin7	G7		Dmin7	G7		C	

Key of A♭

IImin7	V7		IImin7		V7		I
B♭min7	E♭7		B♭min7		A7		A♭

FIG. 18.1. Repetition of the IImin7 V7

PASSING DIMINISHED CHORDS

Very often, it is possible to progress from one "diatonic" chord to another through a "passing" diminished chord. In each case, the function of the diminished chord is to provide smoother and stronger linear motion between the two diatonic chords.

Following is a listing of the most commonly used applications of the passing diminished chord.

a.	I	I°	I
b.	V7	V°	V7
c.	I	♯I°	IImin7
d.	IImin7	♯II°	I_3^6 (3 in the bass)
e.	I_3^6	♭III°	IImin7
f.	IV	♯IV°	I_4^6 (5 in the bass)
g.	I_4^6	♭V°	IV

FIG. 18.2. Passing Diminished Chord Progressions

To be certain that the foregoing is perfectly clear, here is an illustration showing the appearance of each of the preceding patterns in the key of C. Note the chromatic linear motion achieved through the use of the passing diminished chords.

FIG. 18.3. Passing Diminished Chord Progressions in C

To illustrate further, here is a short theme in which the chord progression effectively employs several forms of the passing diminished chord.

FIG. 18.4. Melody with Passing Diminished Chord Progression

DECEPTIVE CADENCE

The normal tendency for any V7 chord is to progress to another chord located a fifth below.

<u>G7 to C</u> ;	<u>G7 to C7</u> ;	<u>G7 to Cmin7</u> ; etc...
5th	5th	5th
Down	**Down**	**Down**

FIG. 18.5. Deceptive Cadence

When a V7 chord is followed by some root motion other than that of down a fifth (or down a half step, if it is a substitute dominant), the result is known as a "deceptive cadence."

Deceptive cadences may generally be classified as being either non-modulating or modulating.

For the present, we shall be concerned exclusively with the first type, i.e., those forms of deceptive cadence that, under normal conditions, usually continue to a conventional cadence in the same key.

The commonly used forms of "non-modulating" deceptive cadence are listed below. In each case, those chords that normally follow the deceptive cadence are also indicated.

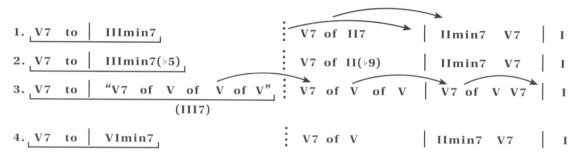

1. <u>V7   to | IIImin7</u>   V7 of II7 | IImin7   V7 | I

2. <u>V7   to | IIImin7(♭5)</u>   V7 of II(♭9) | IImin7   V7 | I

3. <u>V7   to | "V7 of V of V of V"</u>   V7 of V of V | V7 of V V7 | I
                       (III7)

4. <u>V7   to | VImin7</u>   V7 of V | IImin7   V7 | I

FIG. 18.6. Non-Modulating Deceptive Cadences

Figure 18.6 would appear as follows in the key of C:

1. <u>G7 | Emin7</u>   A7 | Dmin7   G7 | C

2. <u>G7 | Emin7♭5</u>   A7(♭9) | Dmin7   G7 | C

3. <u>G7 | E7</u>   A7 | D7   G7 | C

4. <u>G7 | Amin7</u>   D7 | Dmin7   G7 | C

FIG. 18.7. Non-Modulating Deceptive Cadences in C

Although lessons to follow will continue with a further discussion of the techniques of modern harmonic progression, we have by this time progressed far enough to be able to identify and analyze the chord changes that might be used with many standard and popular tunes.

It should be clearly understood at this time that there is no such thing as the correct set of chord changes to a tune. Many different harmonic variations may be used with a given melody depending upon the harmonic style desired (commercial; modern; etc.).

In the following examples, the most commonly used basic changes have been indicated.

FIG. 18.8. Progressions with Deceptive Cadences

ADDITIONAL APPROACH TECHNIQUES

In conjunction with the work on harmonic progression, we now return to the technique of scoring with a discussion of some additional methods of harmonizing approach notes.

These additional approach techniques should be used primarily where the conventional approach note harmonizations do not produce a satisfactory result.

It will necessarily take a certain amount of experimentation to determine just where each type will be most effective, but the interesting results that may be obtained from these various approach harmonizations more than justify the effort.

Independent Lead (Six Types)

1. Lead moves up one whole step. Lower voices move up one half step.

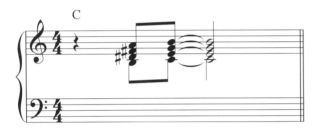

FIG. 18.9. Lead Up Whole Step, Lower Voices Up Half Step

2. Lead moves down one whole step. Lower voices move down one half step.

FIG. 18.10. Lead Down Whole Step, Lower Voices Down Half Step

3. Lead moves up one half step. Lower voices move down one half step.

FIG. 18.11. Lead Up Half Step, Lower Voices Down Half Step

4. Lead moves down one half step. Lower voices move up one half step.

FIG. 18.12. Lead Down Half Step, Lower Voices Up Half Step

5. Lead repeats. Lower voices move down one half step.

FIG. 18.13. Lead Repeats, Lower Voices Down Half Step

6. Lead repeats. Lower voices move up one half step.

FIG. 18.14. Lead Repeats, Lower Voices Up Half Step

In using any of the foregoing forms of independent lead, care should be taken to see that the resulting approach chord forms some logical structure. Do not use an independent lead where the approach chord does not form a logical structure.

Following are some examples illustrating both correct and incorrect usages of independent lead.

Lead moves up one half step.
Lower voices move down one half step.

Lead moves down one half step.
Lower voices move up one half step.

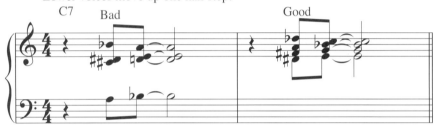

FIG. 18.15. Independent Lead Examples

Diatonic Approach

As the name implies, only scale tones are used in the diatonic approach. Each note of the chord is approached scalewise, with all voices moving in the same direction as the lead.

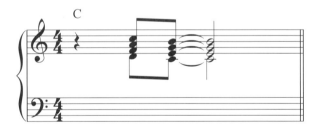

FIG. 18.16. Diatonic Approach

Diatonic approach is usually most effective when it assumes the following appearance:

Approach ⟶ Chord
a) Subdominant ⟶ Tonic
b) Tonic ⟶ Subdominant

Shown below are examples of some effective uses of the diatonic approach.

FIG. 18.17. Effective Uses of Diatonic Approach

NOTE: Any inversion of the above forms may be used.

Parallel Approach

In the parallel approach, all voices move in the same direction and exactly the same interval as the lead, i.e., parallel.

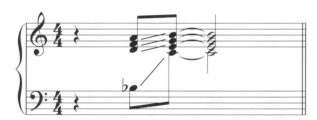

FIG. 18.18. Parallel Approach

Dominant Approach

To use this type of approach, simply harmonize the approach note with some altered form of V7 of the chord being approached. A dominant approach into a C chord (or C7, Cmin, Cmin7, etc.) would consist of some altered form of G7; a dominant approach into any type of B♭ chord would be produced by using an altered form of F7.

FIG. 18.19. Dominant Approach

In order to achieve the most effective result, it is essential that the approaching V7 be used in something other than its original form. Any of the following may be effectively used:

- V7♭5

- V7(♭9)

- V7♯5

- V7(♯9)

- V7♭5(♭9)

- V7♯5(♭9)

- V7♯5(♯9)

Following are several examples of the application of the dominant approach in the block harmonization of a given melody.

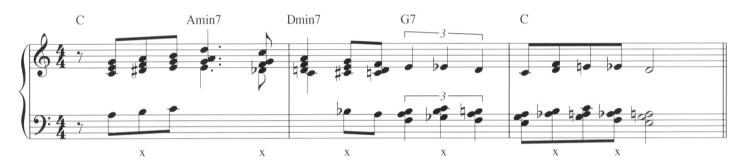

FIG. 18.20. Dominant Approach in Block Harmonizations

In relating the new approach methods described in this lesson to previously discussed approach techniques, it should be noted that most diminished chord harmonizations of scalewise approach notes are simply special applications of the dominant approach, e.g., V7(♭9). Also, chromatic approach notes harmonized "chromatically in all voices" may be considered to be applications of the parallel approach.

Following is an illustration of the four-part block harmonization of a given melody employing these new approach sounds. Naturally this particular example is somewhat overdone for purposes of illustration.

Independent Lead   IL

Diatonic Approach   di

Parallel Approach   par

Dominant Approach   dom

FIG. 18.21. Harmonization with Various Approach Types

In view of the varied approach techniques described in this as well as in former lessons, it should become increasingly obvious to you that there is no single "best method" of harmonizing a given melody. As in the case of the selection of the basic harmonic progression itself, style, instrumentation, and taste will all be determining factors.

More and more your taste, based on your increasing knowledge and experience, will guide you in your selections, and you will find yourself objectively using a particular technique because you are able to associate it with a specific sound.

ASSIGNMENT

1. Notate variations of the passing diminished chord in all keys, similar to figure 18.3.

2. Work out the four forms of deceptive cadence described in this lesson in all keys. (See figure 18.7)

3. Analyze each of the following chord progressions that might be used with the standard tunes indicated. (See figure 18.8)

FIG. 18.22. Practice Progressions

4. (a) Compose one eight-bar chord progression in every key, employing any and all of the harmonic techniques described in lessons 16, 17, and 18.

    (b) Show the analysis of each progression as in problem 3.

5. Work out three practical examples of each of the six types of independent lead. (See figures 18.9 through 18.14.)

6. Notate in all keys the applications of the diatonic approach chord that have been described in this lesson. (See figure 18.17.)

7. Complete a block harmonization of the following melody, using some form of dominant approach at each point marked "x."

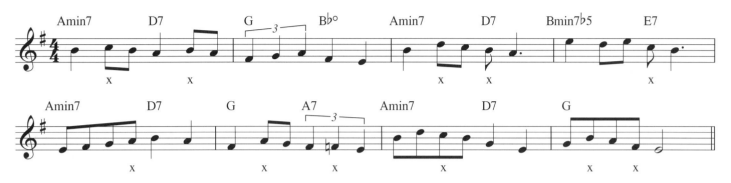

FIG. 18.23. Practice Melody

8. Work out a four-part block harmonization of each of the following given melodies. Employ any of the additional approach methods described in this lesson wherever you feel they may be effective. Indicate each as in figure 18.21.

FIG. 18.24. Practice Melodies

Modulation and Form

As previously stated, some key other than the main key of the composition may be established in the course of a chord progression. One of the commonest and most effective changes is achieved by establishing the relative minor key—i.e., that minor key that has the same signature as its relative major key.

Major Key	Relative Minor Key
C Major	A Minor
A♭ Major	F Minor
D Major	B Minor

FIG. 19.1. Major Keys and Their Relative Minors

The minor key is established by using: IImin7♭5 V7(♭9) Imin:

Minor Key	IImin7♭5	V7(♭9)	Imin
C Major (B Minor)	Bmin7♭5	E7(♭9)	Amin
A♭ Major (F Minor)	Gmin7♭5	C7(♭9)	Fmin
D Major (B Minor)	C♯min7♭5	F♯7(♭9)	Bmin

FIG. 19.2. Establishing Minor with IImin7♭5 V7(♭9) Imin

A smooth transition back to the major key is achieved by using the Imin as a pivot chord as follows:

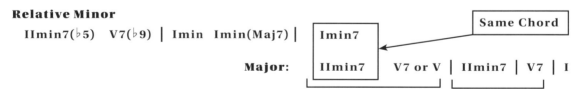

Relative Minor

IImin7(♭5)   V7(♭9) | Imin Imin(Maj7) | Imin7   Same Chord

Major: IImin7   V7 or V | IImin7 | V7 | I

FIG. 19.3. Using Imin as the Pivot Chord

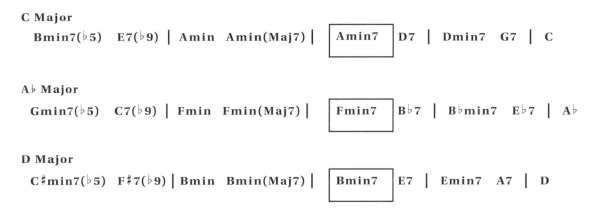

FIG. 19.4. Using Imin as Pivot to Major

Following are two eight-bar chord progressions further illustrating the application of this principle.

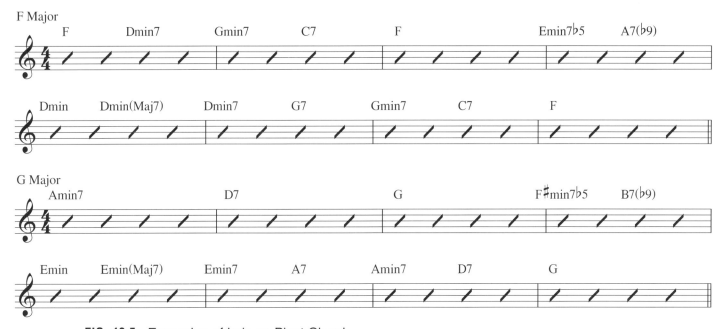

FIG. 19.5. Examples of Imin as Pivot Chord

FORM

Thus far, we have applied the principles of harmonic progression to single eight-bar phrases only. These same principles, however, are still valid in analyzing or constructing the chord progression to a complete tune.

For purposes of this study, we shall discuss the two forms most commonly used in song construction (although there are other variations).

a.	A¹	A²	B	A³

	A¹	A²	B	A³
a.	8 Bars	8 Bars	8 Bars	8 Bars
b.	A¹	B	A²	C
	8 Bars	8 Bars	8 Bars	8 Bars

FIG. 19.6. Common Forms: AABA and ABAC

In type (a), A^1, A^2, and A^3 would be virtually the same, (except for cadential variation in the last two bars of each) while the B theme, also called the "bridge," "channel," or "release," would provide melodic and/or harmonic contrast.

Examples of this (type a) construction may be found in tunes such as:

- "I'm in the Mood for Love"
- "I Cover the Waterfront"
- "Everything Happens to Me"
- "Once in a While"
- etc.

The equally common A^1, B, A^2, C structure (b) may be found in the construction of tunes such as:

- "Deep Purple"
- "Embraceable You"
- "Pennies from Heaven"
- "But Beautiful"
- etc.

It should be understood that the techniques of song construction (actually an involved study in itself) cannot be completely explored in this course. To gain a further understanding of harmonic progression as applied to song structure, it will be necessary for you to devote considerable time to the analysis of popular and standard tunes. (See figures 19.7 and 19.8 and problem 1 of this lesson assignment.)

FIG. 19.7. A¹, A², B, A³ Structure

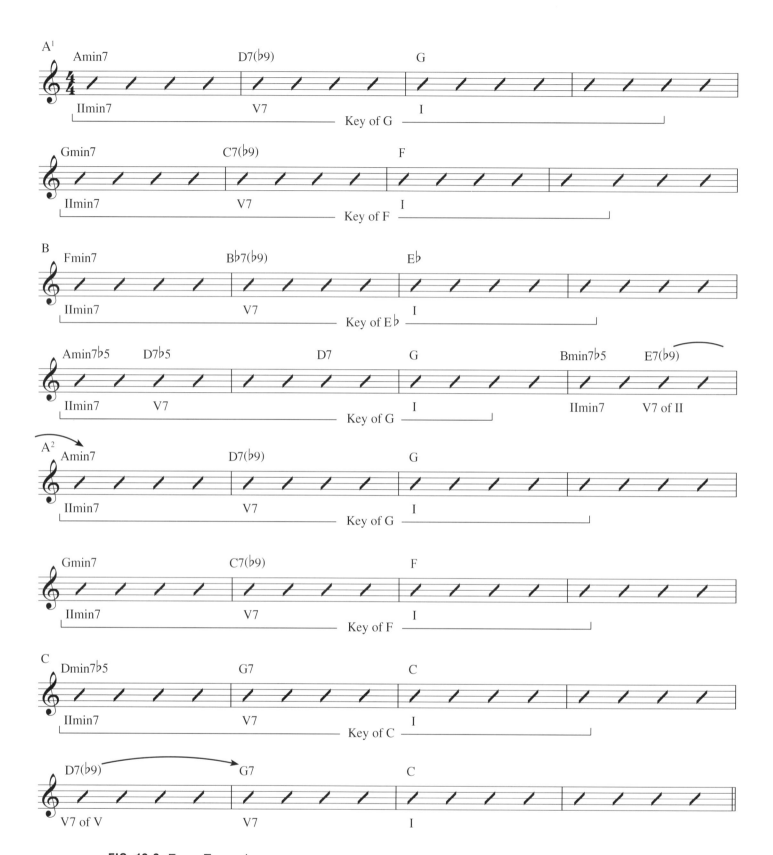

FIG. 19.8. Form Examples

A thorough discussion of the "blues-type" twelve-bar construction will be included in a later lesson.

DECEPTIVE CADENCE

The following forms of deceptive cadence would not normally be found in the chord progression to a standard or popular tune, but rather, would be used to create a special harmonic effect for purposes of modulation or variation in the final cadence.

1.		V7	to	♭VIMaj7	(I)	2.		V7	to	♭IIMaj7	(I)
	Key of C:	G7	"	A♭Maj7	(C)		Key of C:	G7	"	D♭Maj7	(C)
	Key of E♭:	B♭7	"	C♭Maj7	(E♭)		Key of E♭:	B♭7	"	EMaj7	(E♭)

FIG. 19.9. Deceptive Cadences

Where the deceptive cadence is to be followed by a modulation into another key, there is no need to return to the I chord of the original (as in parentheses above).

Modulating Deceptive Cadence

1. Establish a strong melodic cadence on any one of the following degrees of the I chord:

   1, 3, 5, 6, 7, 9

2. Consider this note to be either the 9 or the 11 of some minor seventh chord.

3. Assume this minor seventh chord to be a IImin7, and continue on to the related V7.

4. Cadence directly to the I chord established by this IImin7 V7, or progress as desired to any other key. (See figure 19.10.)

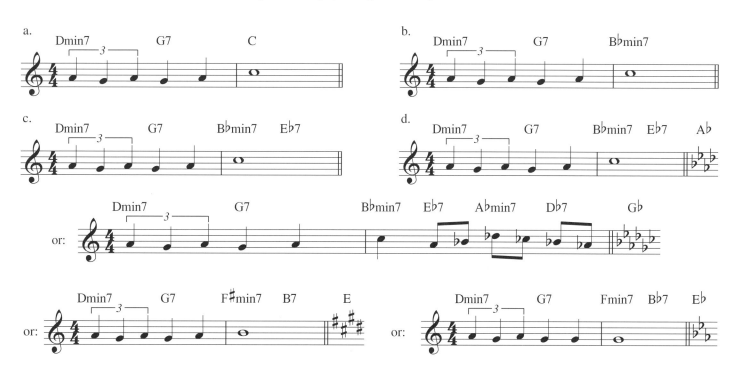

FIG. 19.10. Deceptive Cadence Examples

COMPOSING INTRODUCTIONS AND MODULATIONS

All of the techniques of harmonic progression and melodization discussed in these lessons may be applied to the construction of introductions and modulations.

One harmonic factor that all introductions and modulations will have in common is that the final chord or chords must form some sort of cadence into the first chord of the chorus.

Introductions

Introductions are most commonly four bars in length, but may be two, four, six, or eight bars long.

Generally speaking, introductions may be classified being either *thematic* (based on the material contained in the tune itself) or *non-thematic* (based on new material not contained in the body of the tune).

It is virtually impossible to present an objective coverage of the writing of non-thematic introductions, since so many variations are possible.

To be certain that the principle is clear however, following are some examples of non-thematic introductions.

FIG. 19.11. Examples of Non-Thematic Introductions

Thematic introductions (the most commonly used type) may be based on any rhythmic, melodic, or harmonic motif contained in the arrangement or in the original melody. Again, countless variations are possible in constructing this type of introduction, but it is interesting to note that many are based on some sort of sequential development.

Following are examples of thematic introductions to "I'm in the Mood for Love."

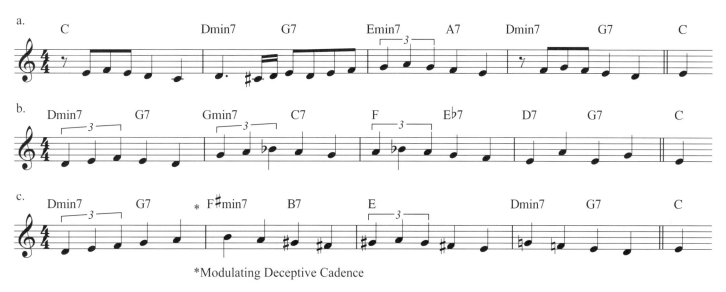

*Modulating Deceptive Cadence

FIG. 19.12. Possible Thematic Introductions to "I'm in the Mood for Love"

Needless to say, the style of the introduction should complement the style of the arrangement by establishing the mood and character of the music to follow.

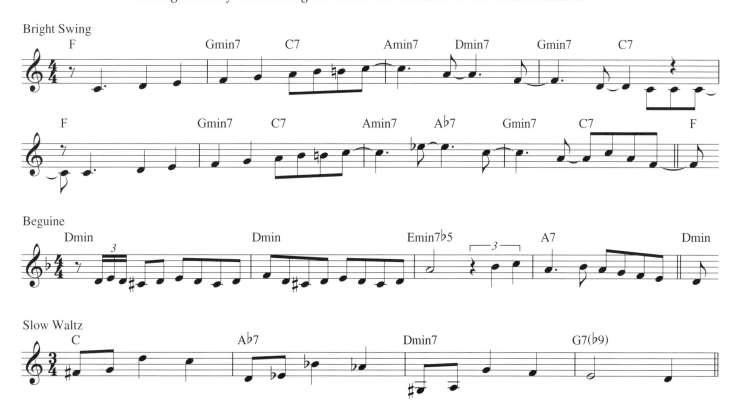

FIG. 19.13. Thematic Introductions to Standards

Modulations

The primary consideration for constructing any modulation is to provide an interesting transition from one key to another. As in the case of introductions, modulations may be based on either thematic or non-thematic material.

There are, of course, many ways in which this transition may be accomplished, and countless variations of the following examples would be possible. Be sure to consider these examples as a starting point for your thinking, rather than an attempt at a complete coverage of the subject of modulation.

FIG. 19.14. Modulation Examples

Principles of harmonic progression as discussed in lessons 16 through 19 have been used exclusively in constructing the modulations and introductions used in this lesson.

ASSIGNMENT

1. Analyze the chord changes to each of the standard progressions included at the end of the assignment. (See figures 19.7 and 19.8.)

2. Compose one eight-bar progression in every key, establishing the relative minor key at some point in the progression. (See figure 19.4.)

3. Notate the following deceptive cadences in every key.

   a. V7   to   ♭VIMaj7   (I)

   b. V7   to   ♭IIMaj7(I)

4. Utilizing the principle of modulating deceptive cadence as described in this lesson, construct a modulation of any length from the key of C into each of the eleven other keys. Compose a melody and chord progression for each of the eleven modulations.

5. Compose a thematic introduction of any desired length (melody and chords) to each of the following standard tunes. (See figure 19.12.)

   - You Are Too Beautiful
   - Can't Help Lovin' That Man
   - Body and Soul
   - I Only Have Eyes for You
   - How High the Moon
   - Deep Purple

   - September Song
   - Somebody Loves Me
   - Someone to Watch Over Me
   - I Cover the Waterfront
   - Jeepers Creepers
   - Gone with the Wind

NOTE: In the event that you are not familiar with any of the foregoing tunes, simply substitute tunes of your own choice.

6. Compose both the melody and the chord progression for twelve non-thematic introductions (one in every key) in each of the following styles. These introductions may be of any desired length. (See figure 19.13.)

   a. Waltz

   b. Slow Ballad

   c. Bright or Medium Swing

   d. Beguine (or any other Latin-American beat)

7. Construct a modulation of any desired length leading from:

   a. C to A♭
   b. B♭ to D♭
   c. A♭ to A
   d. E♭ to G

   e. D to B
   f. G to F
   g. G♭ to B♭
   h. D♭ to G♭

   i. F to B♭
   j. A to E♭
   k. B♭ to C
   l. C to E♭

Any of the techniques of melodization and chord progression discussed in these lessons may be used. The modulations may be either non-thematic (if based on specific tunes) or thematic.

8. Using any standard tune of your choice:

    a. Transpose the melody to a key suitable for a five-part brass soli in open position.

    b. Compose a percussive, rhythmic improvisation of the original melody.

    c.   Score for:

        I   B♭ Trumpet

        II   B♭ Trumpet

        III B♭ Trumpet

        I   B♭ Trombone

        II   B♭ Trombone

In scoring problem 8, try to make use of inner-voice tensions as discussed in lesson 15.

Progression 1

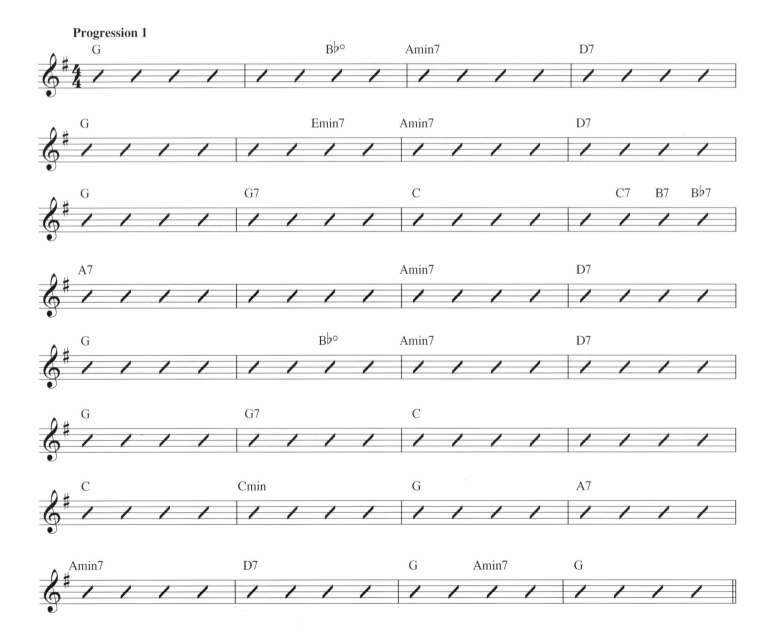

FIG. 19.15. Practice Progressions

Reharmonization

The principles of chord progression as discussed in the past few lessons may be applied effectively in the *reharmonization* of a given chord progression. Reharmonization of a given progression may be necessary or desirable for either or both of the following reasons:

1. to correct chord changes that, for one reason or another, are incorrect on the existing piano part or lead sheet

2. to provide harmonic motion through the use of added chords, or harmonic interest through the application of substitute chords.

Both of these principles have been considered in the reharmonization of the following chord progressions. In each case, the basic chord has been taken from the printed piano copy. Needless to say, the melodic line has been carefully considered in constructing the reharmonized progression.

To derive the maximum benefit from these examples;

1. Study each carefully, being certain that the logic behind each of the reharmonizations is clear to you.

2. Play (or have someone else play) the melody, first with the original chord progression, and then with the reharmonized chord progression. Listen closely to the sound of each and try to associate the harmonic techniques involved with the resulting musical sound.

Progression 1

Progression 2

Original

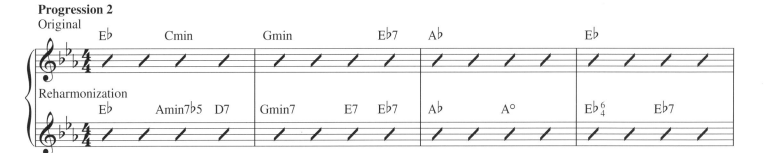

Reharmonization

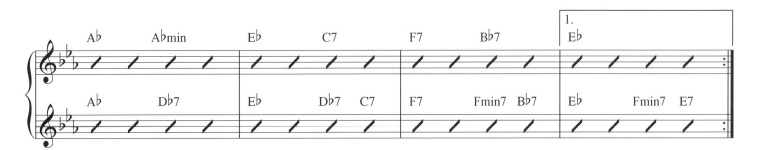

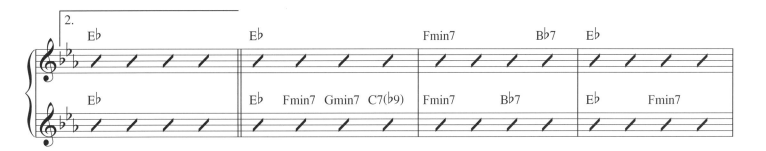

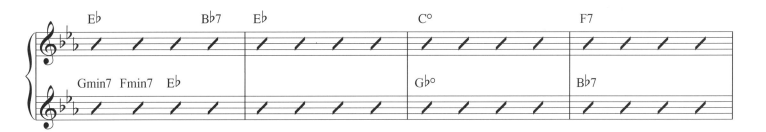

Progression 3

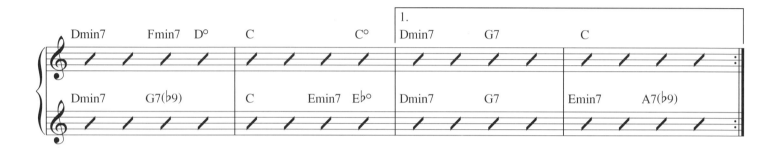

Progression 4
Original

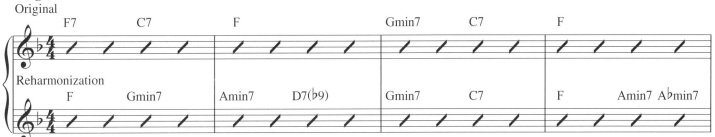

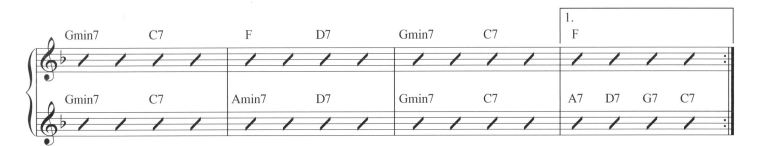

Progression 5

FIG. 20.1. Progressions and Reharmonizations

"BLUES"

The term "blues" has come to represent almost any twelve-bar harmonic phrase regardless of its resemblance to the simple traditional blues outline.

In this discussion, it is not our purpose to analyze the historical development of the "blues" nor to establish strict definitions that will enable us to determine whether or not a certain twelve-bar phrase may or may not be accurately defined as "blues."

Rather, using the traditional blues pattern as a guide, we shall try to develop related twelve-bar phrases using the techniques of harmonization and reharmonization as discussed in previous lessons.

The basic traditional blues chord progression consisted of:

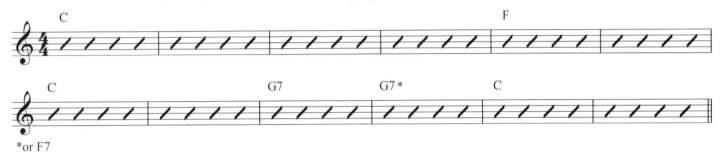

*or F7

FIG. 20.2. Blues Form

Following are several examples of variations on the original blues progression. Notice that the essential harmonic elements of the traditional twelve-bar blues have been retained in each example:

Bar 1:   Tonic

Bar 5:   Subdominant

Bar 7:   Tonic

Bar 9:   Dominant (or IImin7 to V7)

Bar 11:   Tonic

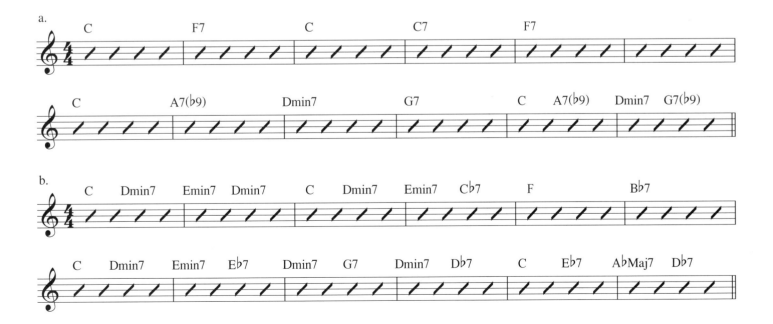

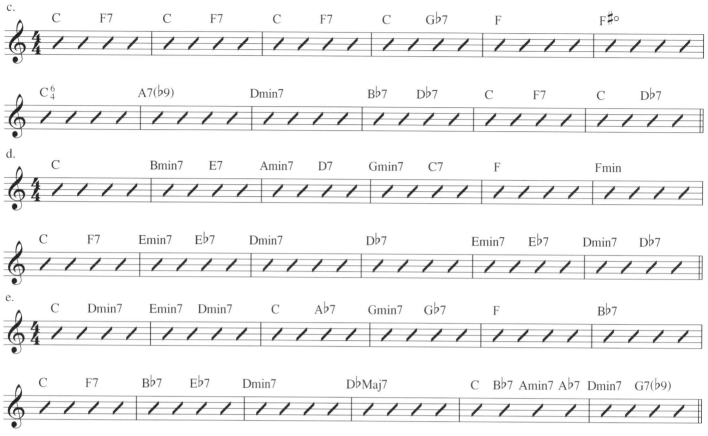

FIG. 20.3. Blues Variations

By applying previously discussed melodic techniques to these harmonic progressions, we may now construct some original blues compositions.

An important factor to be considered, if a real "blues" feeling is desired, is the incorporation in the melody of the so-called "blues notes,"—the ♭3 and the ♭7 of the major scale.

FIG. 20.4. Blues Notes and Sample Melody

Following are examples of melodized blues chord changes:

FIG. 20.5. Blues Melodies

ASSIGNMENT

1. Reharmonize each of the following chord progressions. In each case, write out the melodic line first, and consider it carefully as you rewrite the given chord progression. The finished reharmonization should appear as follows:

Progression 3

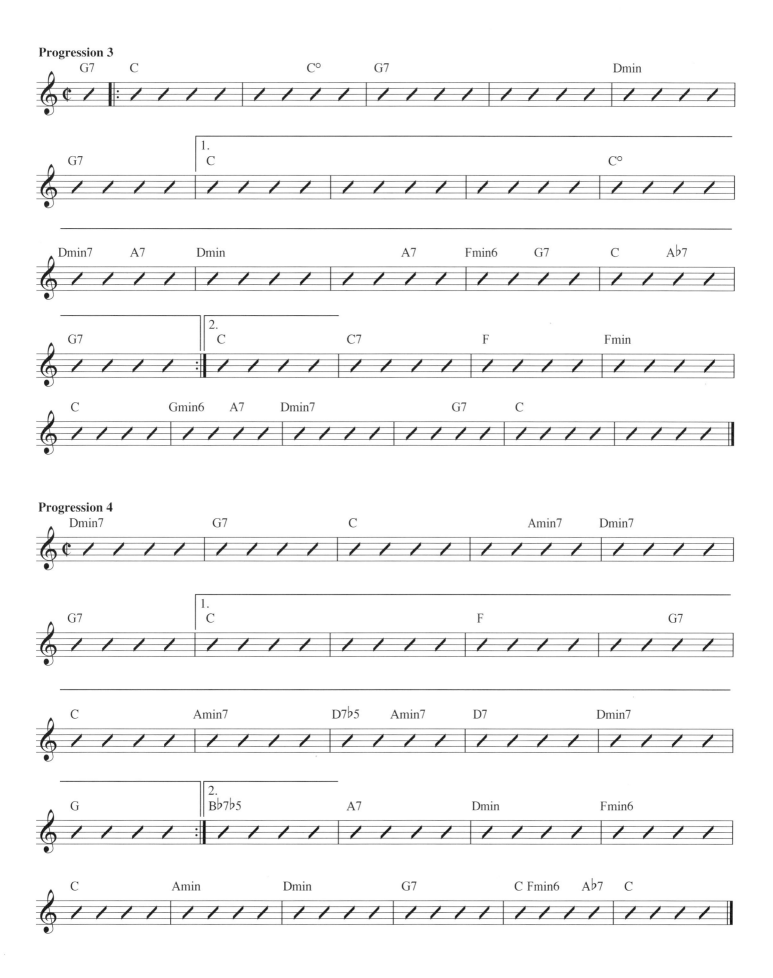

Progression 5

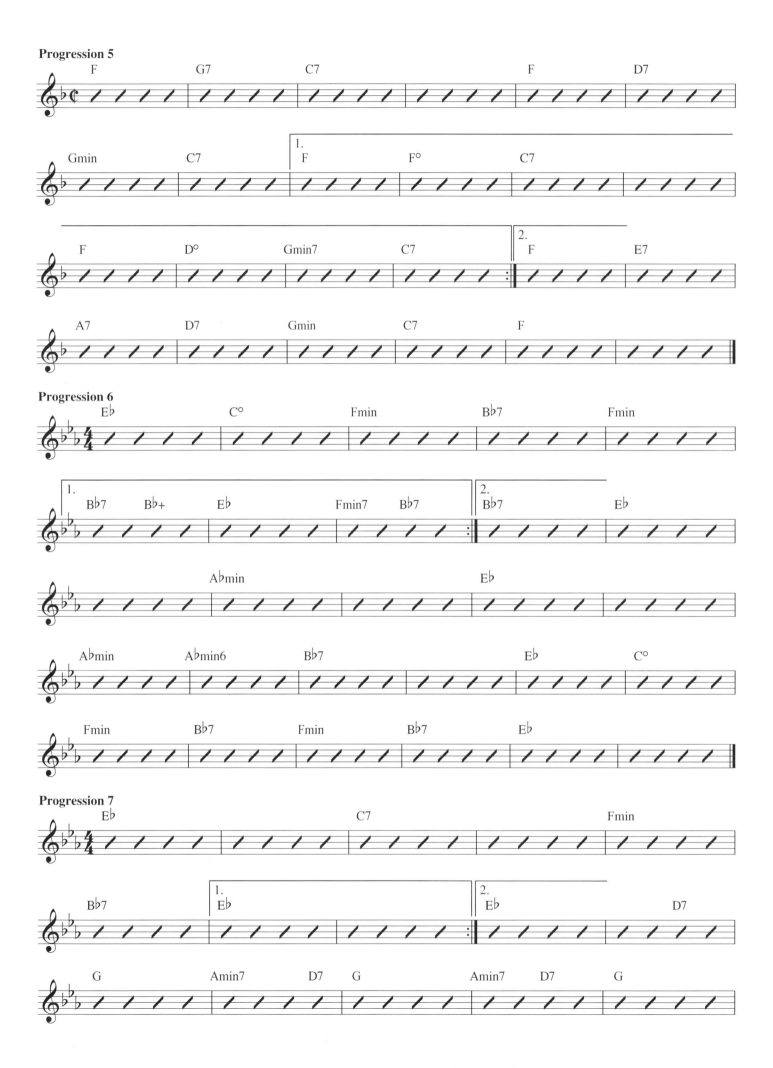

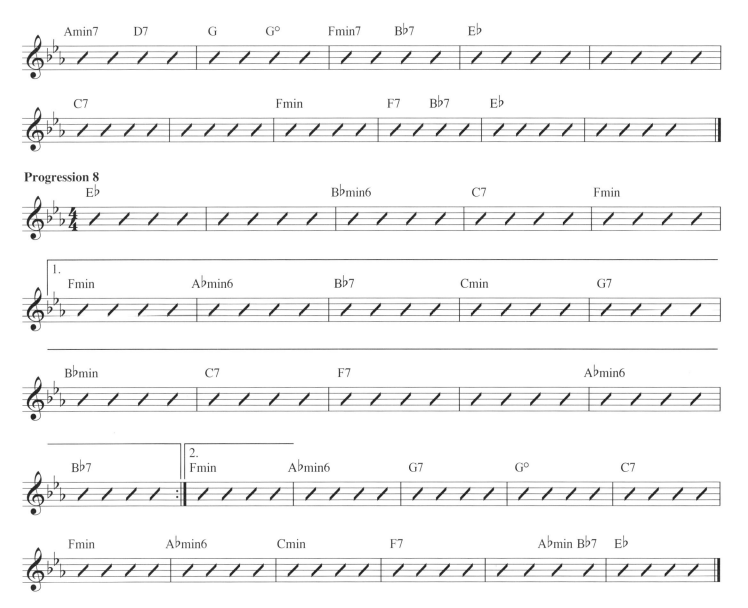

FIG. 20.6. Practice Progressions

Alternatively, substitute standard tune progressions of your own choice.

2. Compose two "blues" chord progressions in every key. Each may be either traditional or modern in feeling.

3. Compose a melodic line to any ten of the chord progressions resulting from problem 2. Achieve a "blues" feeling through the utilization of the lowered 3 and lowered 7 as described in this lesson.

4. Using any of the blues compositions from problem 3, set up a score for each of the following musical situations (using a different original for each problem):

a.   Original blues: Sax soli, five-part block A, A, T, T, B

FIG. 20.7. Score Setup

b.   Original blues: Sax unison and brass background (closed or open): three trumpets, two trombones.

FIG. 20.8. Score Setup

c.   Original blues: Trumpet solo and sax background (closed or open): A, A, T, T, B

FIG. 20.9. Score Setup

d.   Original blues: Brass soli, five-part (open or closed)

FIG. 20.10. Score Setup

5. Using one of your original blues compositions as a guide, set up a score as follows using layout as shown below:

Brass: three trumpets, two trombones

FIG. 20.11. Score Setup

Saxes: A, A, T, T, B

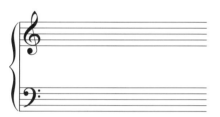

FIG. 20.12. Score Setup

Chord progression

FIG. 20.13. Score Setup

a. First twelve bars: original melody, sax unison (or octaves)

b. Second twelve bars: original melody, sax unison and brass background (cup mutes)

c. Third twelve bars: improvised melody, trumpet solo and sax background (closed or open)

d. Fourth twelve bars: improvised melody, trombone solo and sax background, A, A, T, T, B (closed)

e. Fifth twelve bars: original melody, brass soli (closed or open)

f. Sixth twelve bars: original melody, sax unison and brass background (cup mutes)

NOTE: the successful completion of problems 4 and 5 will depend on:

1. the musical quality of the original composition; try to select those that sound best to you.

2. your ability to visualize the timbre and individual characteristics of each of the instruments or instrumental sections for which you are writing; try to literally "hear" as you write.

The Rhythm Section

In this lesson, we discuss the four instruments of the rhythm section and their function in the orchestra.

DRUMS (PERCUSSION)

The dance-band or jazz drummer makes use of a number of different percussion instruments.

    a. Bass Drum. Notated on the bottom space with stems down (*bass clef).

FIG. 21.1. Bass Drum

    b. Snare Drum. Notated in the third space with stems up. "Snares on" will produce the sound normally associated with the snare drum. "Snares off" will result in a more muffled "tom-tom"-like sound.

FIG. 21.2. Snare Drum

    c. Cymbals. Notated in the fourth space with stems up. Special note shapes as follows:

FIG. 21.3. Cymbals

d. Tom-Tom (one or several). Notated as snare drum but with "T.T." indicated before the tom-tom passage.

Following is a list of abbreviations and expression marks commonly associated with drumming and their meanings:

B.D.	Bass Drum
S.D.	Snare Drum
T.T.	Tom-Tom
Cym	Cymbal
R.S.	Rim Shot
St	Sticks
Br	Brushes
∕.	Repeat Preceding Bar
∕∕.	Repeat Preceding Two Bars
	Roll

FIG. 21.4. Abbreviations in Percussion Notation

NOTE: a drum roll should always have an ending attack; i.e.;

Remember that a drummer's primary function is to provide a steady rhythmic foundation for the band and that he or she should depart from this only for occasional special effect (e.g., to provide fill-ins between ensemble passages, to emphasize percussive orchestral figures, etc.).

Following are some of the basic beats commonly used by the dance-band drummer.

FIG. 21.5. Basic Beats

In using each of the above, the term "ad lib" is usually noted on the drum part allowing the drummer freedom in following the arrangement. It is also customary to indicate the predominant solo or section activity on the drum part.

NOTE: The tendency will always be to over-arrange for the drummer. Unless some specific effect is desired, give the drummer as little as possible to read.

STRING BASS (BASS FIDDLE)

In dance-band or jazz writing, the bass is usually plucked (*pizzicato, pizz.*), but may be used with bow for special effect (*arco*).

The bass, naturally enough, is notated in the bass clef and written one octave higher than it actually sounds. The four strings are tuned as follows:

FIG. 21.6. Open Bass Strings

The practical range of the bass (transposed) is shown in figure 21.7, but higher notes are possible and are used for special effect in solo passages.

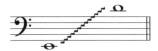

FIG. 21.7. Bass Range

The following illustrations will serve as a guide in the writing of bass parts:

1.   One chord per bar.

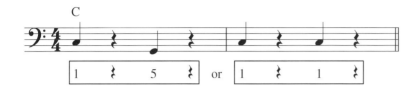

FIG. 21.8. Bass Line for One Chord Per Bar: Continuing Harmony

2.   When a I chord is followed by its V7.

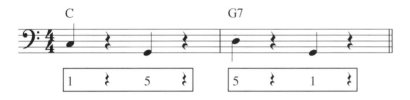

FIG. 21.9. Bass Line for One Chord Per Bar: I to V7

3.   Two chords per bar.

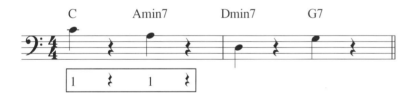

FIG. 21.10. Bass Line for Two Chords Per Bar

4.   Rests may be replaced by repeated notes.

FIG. 21.11. Repeated Notes

5.   Degrees 1 5 may be used instead of 1 1.

FIG. 21.12. Using 1 and 5

6. Chord or scale notes other than 1 and 5 (usually 3 or 7) may be used to provide melodic motion.

FIG. 21.13. Adding Melodic Motion with Scale Notes

7. Where the root motion of the chord progression moves down a fifth, a passing ♭5 may be used on either dominant 7 or minor 7 chords to provide chromatic bass motion (5 ♭5 1).

FIG. 21.14. Passing ♭5

The preceding must necessarily be considered as a general outline, and other techniques may be used where they appear to be musically justified.

GUITAR

When used for single-string passages, the guitar is written one octave higher than it actually sounds. The six strings of the guitar are tuned as follows:

FIG. 21.15. Open Guitar Strings: Not transposed.

The practical solo range of the guitar (transposed) is:

FIG. 21.16. Guitar Range and Transposition

In rhythm work, the actual voicing of the chord is normally left to the guitarist, with the arranger simply indicating the chord symbols and the number of beats each chord is to occupy.

FIG. 21.17. Chord Chart for Rhythm Guitar

Special rhythmic effects may be indicated as in the following illustration:

FIG. 21.18. Notating Rhythmic Effects

PIANO

The arranger may use either of two styles in writing piano parts, depending upon:

1. the style of playing desired, and;

2. the demands of the arranging assignment

The simplest type of piano part, and that which allows the pianist the most freedom, simply consists of a combination of the bass and chords. The piano player is expected to create an appropriate rhythmical background from this outline.

Following is an illustration of a piano part of this type.

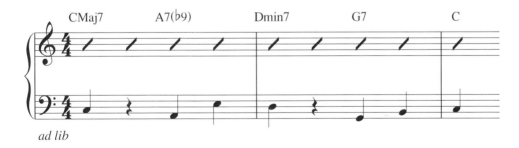

ad lib

FIG. 21.19. Piano Part with Bass and Chords

It is also desirable in certain situations to indicate the melodic line in cue form to guide the piano player as he improvises a background.

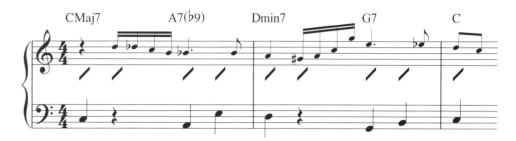

FIG. 21.20. Melodic Cue Notation

Although somewhat more demanding of the arranger, the following type of piano part should be used when:

1. a specific piano effect is desired, or

2. the pianist is unable to spontaneously create his own part from the chord symbols and bass line.

In writing this type of piano part, try to consider the following principles:

1. Let the left hand duplicate the bass part.

2. Consider the technical limitations of the pianist.

3. Write no higher than $\begin{array}{c}\text{♭o}\end{array}$ in rhythmic passages.

4. Keep smooth voice leading between adjacent chords in the right hand.

5. Treat the piano as a rhythm instrument; it is not necessary for the piano part to outline every accent and nuance of the ensemble.

6. In writing "boom-chick" style piano parts, use mostly three-part chords in the right hand (usually 1-3-5 with triads, and 1-3-7 or 3-5-7 with seventh chords).

Following is an example of a piano part of this type:

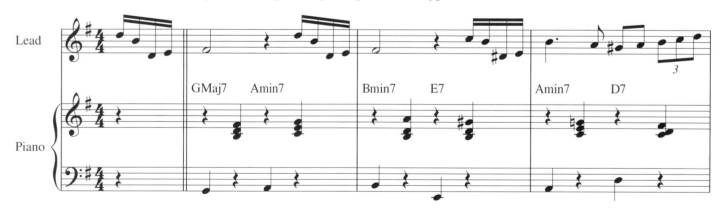

FIG. 21.21. Boom-Chick Piano Part

An effective device in creating full sounding piano backgrounds is the "thumb counter-melody." In this technique, the lowest voice of the three-part harmonic continuity in the right hand forms a sustained melodic counter line, while the upper two voices attack on beats 2 and 4. (Left hand attacks on beats 1 and 3.)

Depending upon where the natural counter line falls, the counter melody may sometimes occur in the top voice of the right hand, while the lower two voices provide the rhythmic accents on beats 2 and 4.

The following example illustrates this principle of "counter-melody."

FIG. 21.22. Counter-Melody

The foregoing should not be interpreted as an exhaustive analysis of the instruments of the rhythm section. A thorough study of each of the instruments individually would be necessary for this, and the scope of this course does not allow for concentrated coverage of any one instrument. Rather, the information given in lesson 21 is intended to serve as a general guide in enabling you to arrange for the rhythm section.

A careful study of the following examples illustrating various rhythm section styles is recommended.

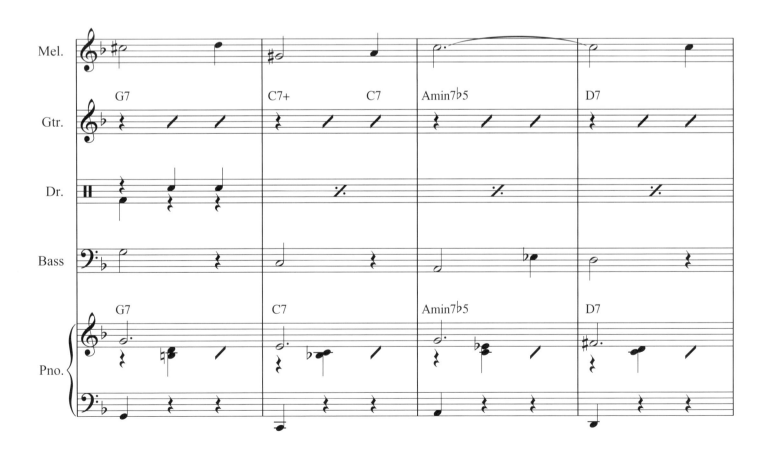

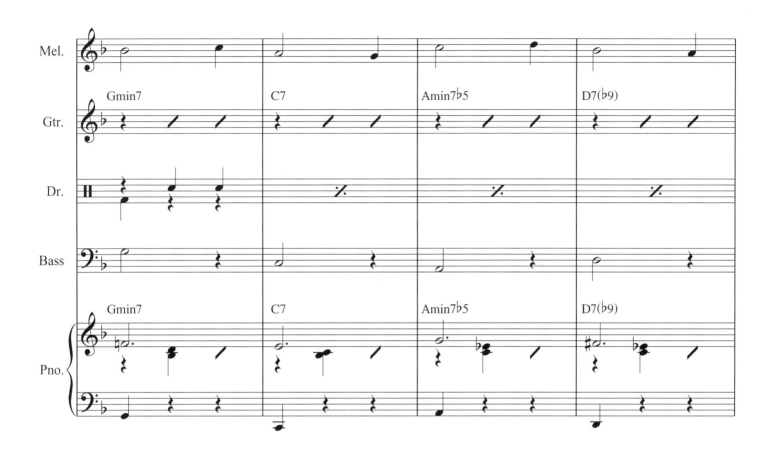

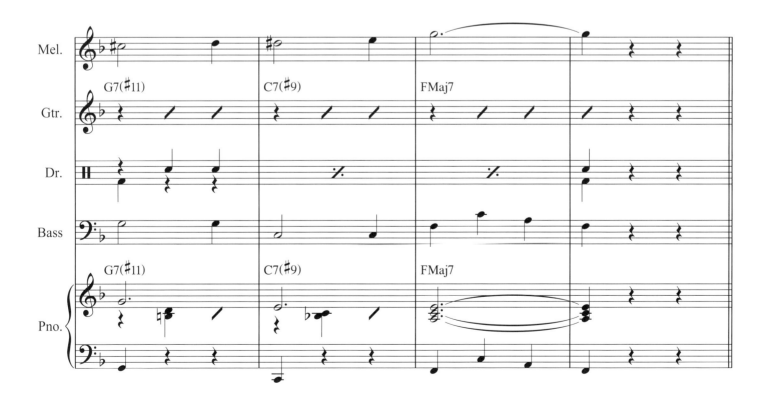

FIG. 21.23. Rhythm Section Examples

ASSIGNMENT

1. Following are the common chord changes to some standard tunes.

   a. Correct and/or reharmonize the given chord changes.

   b. Score parts for the rhythm section as follows:

FIG. 21.24. Score for Rhythm Section

In the event that any of the indicated tunes are not familiar to you, simply substitute standard tunes of your own choice.

Progression 3

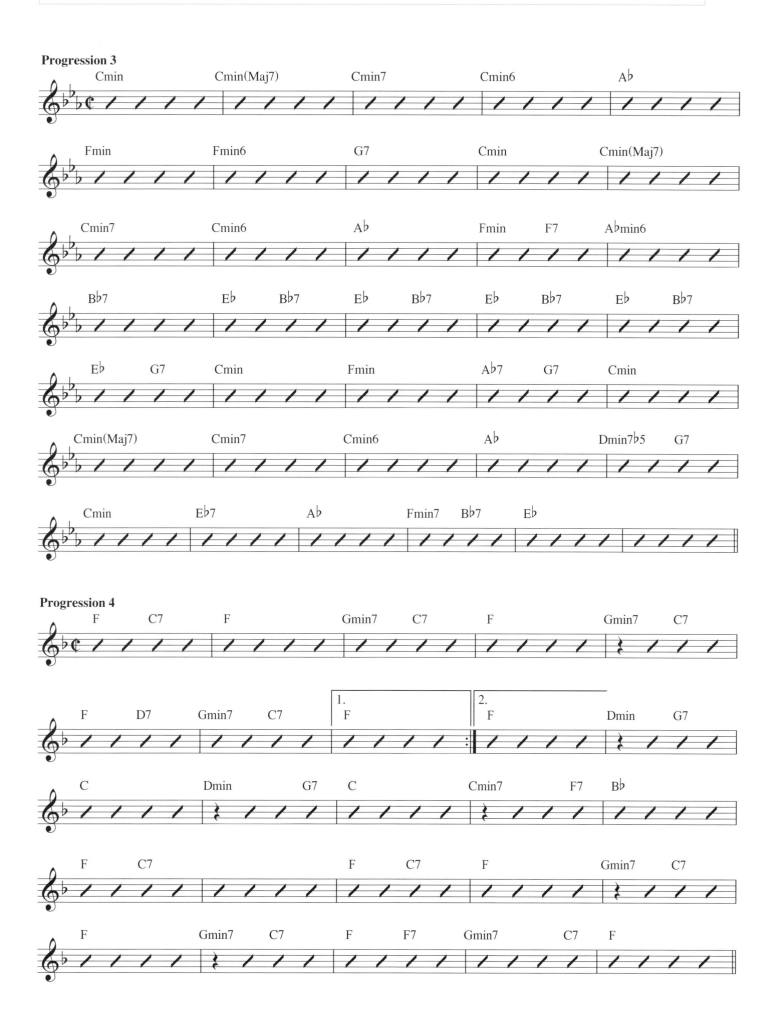

Progression 4

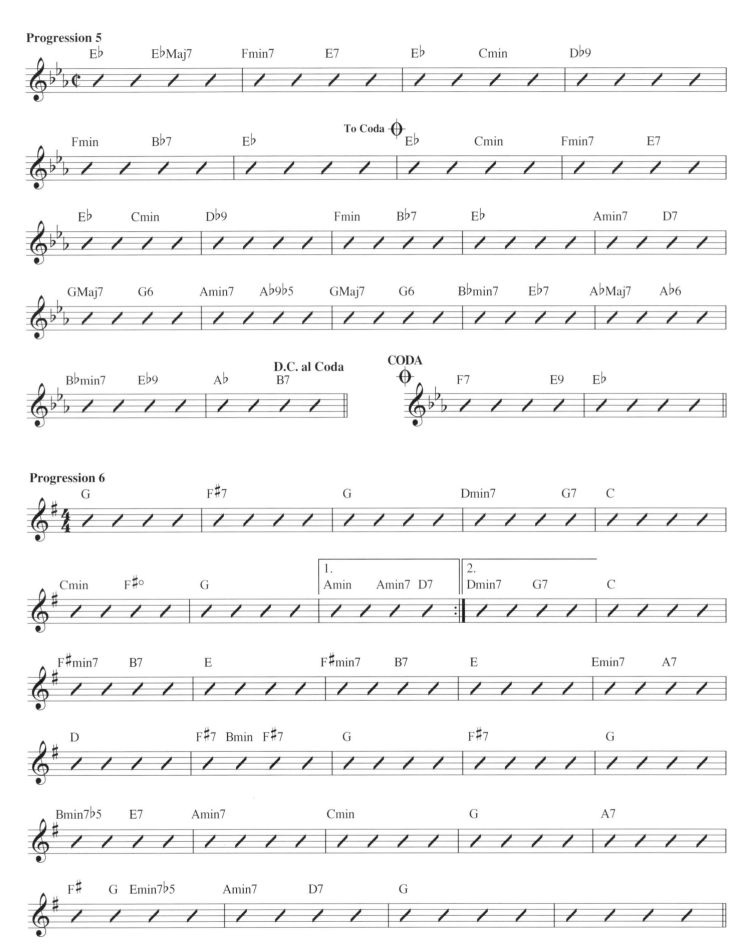

FIG. 21.25. Practice Progressions

2. Score each of the following melodies as indicated. If range of given melody seems impractical for indicated instrumentation, transpose to a more suitable key.

Melody: Sax Unison
Background: Five Brass (Trp., Trp., Trp., Tbn., Tbn.)
Rhythm: Guitar, Drums, Bass, Piano

Ballad

Melody: Five-Part Sax Soli (A, A, T, T, B)
Rhythm: Guitar, Drums, Bass, Piano

Swing

Melody: Five-Part Brass Soli (Trp., Trp., Trp., Tbn., Tbn.)
Rhythm: Guitar, Drums, Bass, Piano

Swing

Melody:	Trumpet Solo
Background:	Five Saxes (A, A, T, T, B)
Rhythm:	Guitar, Drums, Bass, Piano

Melody:	Sax Unison
Background :	Five Brass (Trp., Trp., Trp., Tbn., Tbn.)
Rhythm:	Guitar, Drums, Bass, Piano

Suggested Piano Accompaniment Patterns

Melody:	Four-Part Trombone Soli
Rhythm:	Guitar, Drums, Bass, Piano

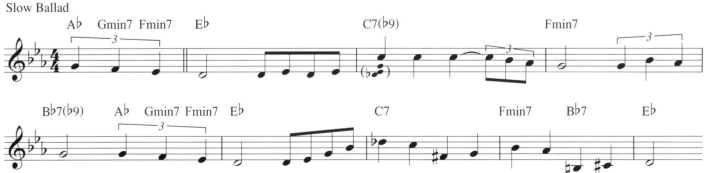

FIG. 21.26. Practice Melodies

3. Using any standard tune of your choice:

   (a) Transpose to key suitable for indicated instrumentation. (if necessary)

   (b) Reharmonize and/or correct chord changes.

   (c) Make any desired rhythmic and/or melodic changes.

   (d) Score as follows:

   - Melody: Trumpet Solo

   - Background: Five Saxes (A, A, T, T, B)

   - Rhythm: Guitar, Drums, Bass, Piano

4. (a) Compose thematic introductions to each of the tunes listed in problem 1 (or any six standard tunes).

   (b) Score each introduction for rhythm section plus any one of the following:

   - Brass Soli

   - Sax Soli

   - Brass Solo (or Unison); Sax Background

   - Sax Solo (or Unison); Brass Background

NOTES

Small Band Writing

TWO HORNS

When scoring for two melody instruments, any of the following may be used:

1. Unison or octaves

2. Duet style (i.e., two-part soli)

3. Melody and counter-melody

Unison

The decision as to whether to use unison or octaves is largely dependent upon the instruments being used and the range of the melodic line. Either is effective.

Duet Style

Try to observe the following principles in writing a two-part soli:

1. If the lead voice is a chord note, use a chord note in second voice. If the lead voice is an approach note, use an approach in the second voice.

FIG. 22.1. Lead Chord Tone vs. Approach Note

2. Try to use intervals of thirds and sixths as much as possible. Consecutive thirds and sixths may be freely used, but avoid using seconds, fourths, fifths, and sevenths consecutively.

FIG. 22.2. Favoring Consecutive Thirds and Sixths

3. When using intervals other than thirds or sixths, try to have them lead directly to either a third or sixth through contrary or oblique motion.

contrary motion   voices move in opposite directions
oblique motion   one voice moves while the other voice sustains or repeats

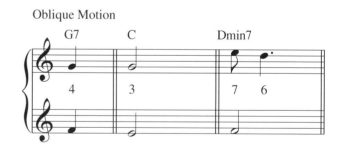

FIG. 22.3. Contrary and Oblique Motion

Figure 22.4 is an example of a given melody harmonized in duet style.

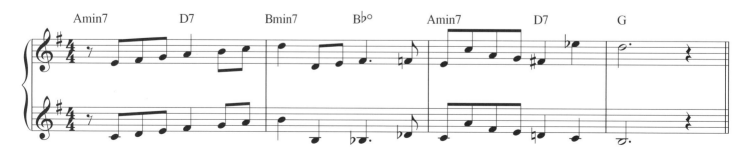

FIG. 22.4. Duet-Style Harmonization

Melody and Counter-Melody

The *melody and counter-melody technique* is certainly the most modern form of
two-part writing, and usually the most interesting musically. A detailed explanation
of counter-melody writing has been included in that part of the course dealing with
backgrounds.

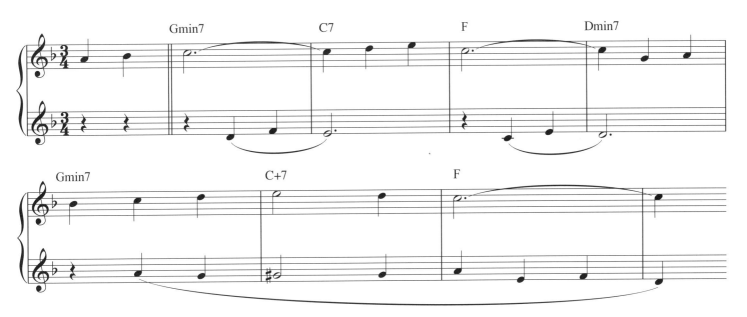

FIG. 22.5. Melody and Counter-Melody

It is, of course, possible to intermingle the three techniques described thus far.

FIG. 22.6. Combining Techniques

THREE HORNS

In scoring for three melody instruments, any of the following may be effectively used:

1. Unison (or octaves)

FIG. 22.7. Unison

2. Unison melody with solo counter-melody

FIG. 22.8. Unison Melody with Solo Counter-Melody

3. Solo melody with unison counter-melody

FIG. 22.9. Solo Melody with Unison Counter-Melody

4.   Solo melody with harmonized counter-melody

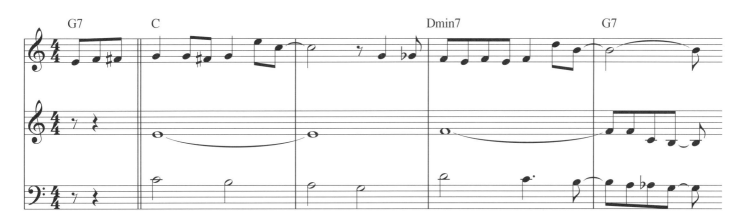

FIG. 22.10. Solo Melody with Harmonized Counter-Melody

5.   Duet-style soli with solo counter-melody

FIG. 22.11. Duet-Style Soli with Solo Counter-Melody

6.   Three-part soli. In setting up a soli voicing for three horns, try to observe the
     following:

     a.   Every chordal harmonization should include the third.

     b.   Every dominant 7 chord harmonization should include the 7.

     c.   Altered chords (♯5, ♭5, ♭9, etc.) should include the altered function.

     d.   Do not use "Hi" and related "Lo" in the same voicing.

     e.   Harmonize chord notes, approach notes, etc., as they would normally be
          harmonized in a four-part voicing, omitting the least important note.

Three-Part Soli Voicings

Major or Minor							
Lead	1	3	5	6	7	9	
Under-Voices	5 6 3 3	1 1 7 5 6 5	3 3 (9) 1 7 (6)	3 5 1 3	5 3 3 1	7 6 5 3 3 3	
Dominant 7							
Lead	1	3	5	7	9	11	13
Under-Voices	7 3	1 9 7 7 7 5	3 (♭9) 7 (7)	5 3 3 1	7 (13)* 3 (3)	9 7 7 5	3 (3)* (♭9)* 7 (♭9) (7)
Minor 7							
Lead	1	3	5	7	9	11	
Under-Voices	7 5 3 3	1 7 5 5	3 3 1 7	5 3 3 1	7 5 3 3	1 7 5 5	
Augmented 7 and Diminished 7							
Lead plus any two other chord notes.							

*Irregular, but effective.

FIG. 22.12. Three-Part Soli Voicings

In any of the voicings shown in figure 22.12, the two under-voices may be inverted to form open position.

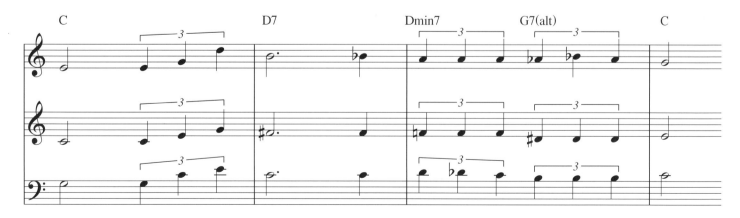

FIG. 22.13. Open Position

In addition to its application to combo writing, the technique of three-part soli writing may also be used when scoring for any three-horn section (three saxes, three trumpets, three trombones, etc.).

7. Three independent lines. This is one of the most modern, most difficult and most interesting methods for scoring for three horns. The technique is as follows:

    a. Set up melodic lead.

    b. Compose a counter-melody.

    c. Compose an additional counter-melody by:

        (i) establishing "missing" chordal functions at strong points of attack, and

        (ii) filling in with non-conflicting melodic motion.

It will, necessarily, take a reasonable amount of experience to become proficient at this type of writing.

FIG. 22.14. Combination of Techniques

Again, in actual practice, any of the forms of three-part writing described in this lesson may be freely intermingled.

FOUR HORNS

Below are listed the most common voicings used in scoring for four melody instruments. Needless to say, many other effective combinations are possible, and experimentation with various voicings is certainly advisable.

1. Unison (or octaves)

2. Four-part soli (closed or open)

3. Three-part soli (doubled lead)

4. Coupled two-part soli

5. Solo melody with three-part background, etc.

Following are illustrations of these four-part horn voicing techniques.

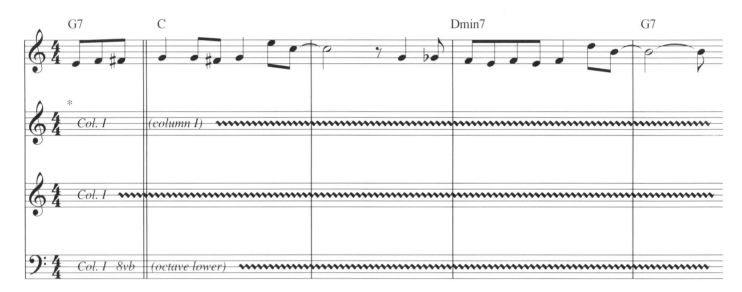

FIG. 22.15. Unison. *Col.* means that this staff shares the notes of the notated staff indicated.

FIG. 22.16. Four-Part Soli. *Dominant approach; open position for smoother leading in under-voices.

FIG. 22.17. Three-Part Soli (Doubled Lead)

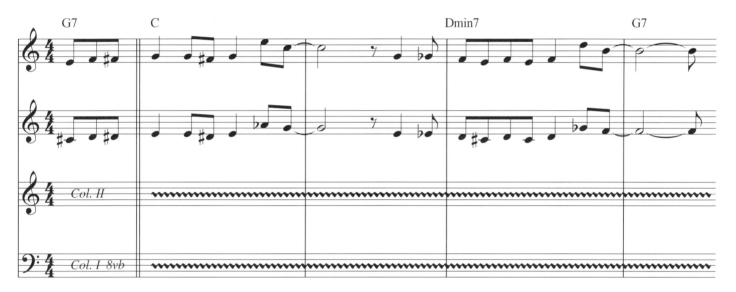

FIG. 22.18. Coupled Two-Part Soli. Doubling may occur in different octaves, depending upon instrumentation and range of melody.

FIG. 22.19. Solo Melody with Three-Part Background

Numerous variations of the basic principles outlined in this lesson are possible when working with five, six, or more horns.

Following are some suggested voicings that are commonly used, but it is advisable that you experiment as much as possible with other combinations.

Remember, also, that a very effective technique in big-band scoring is the use of a "small-band" within the "big-band."

FIVE HORNS

1. Trumpet: Solo melody

   Four saxes: Four-part background

2. Four saxes: Soli

   Trumpet: Solo obligato

3. Two trombones, two tenors, bari: Five-part soli

4. Alto, alto: Duet

   Tenor, tenor, bari: Three-part background

5. Three trumpets: Three-part soli

   Two trombones: Unison counter-melody

6. Trumpet (cup), clarinet: Two-part soli

   Trumpet (cup), clarinet, tenor: Solo counter-melody

7. Trumpet, alto, tenor, trombone, bari: Five-part soli

   Etc.

SIX HORNS

1. Trumpet: Solo melody

   Five saxes: Five-part background

2. Three trumpets, three trombones: Six-part soli (Four-part soli, doubled lead and second voice)

3. Three trombones: Three-part soli

   Tenor, tenor, bari: Three-part background

4. Three trumpets (cup), trombone (cup): Four-part soli

   Two trombones (open): Unison counter-melody

5. Guitar, clarinet (lead), three clarinets, tenor (doubled lead): Five-part soli

6. Trumpet: Solo obligato

   Trombone: Solo melody

   Alto, tenor, tenor, bari: Four-part background

   Etc.

ASSIGNMENT

1. Given is an eight-bar melody. Score it for each of the given instrumentations in each of the indicated styles.

   NOTE: Where musically advisable, original melody may be altered slightly or transposed to a different key.

FIG. 22.20. Practice Melody

   (a) Trumpet, alto: Two-part soli

   (b) Trumpet: melody

       Tenor: Counter-melody

   (c) Three trombones: Three-part soli

   (d) Trumpet: Solo melody

       Alto, tenor: Two-part background

   (e) Trumpet, tenor, bari: Three independent lines

   (f) Trombone, trombone, tenor, bari: Four-part soli

   (g) Clarinet: Solo melody

       Three trombones: Three-part background

2. Using any of the techniques described in this lesson, score any standard tune of your choice for the following four ensembles.

Ensemble 1 (2 Winds)	Ensemble 2 (3 Winds)	Ensemble 3 (5 Winds)	Ensemble 4 (6 Winds)
Trumpet	Trumpet	Trumpet	Trumpet
Tenor Sax	Tenor Sax	Alto Sax	Trumpet
	Trombone	Tenor Sax	Trombone
		Trombone	Alto Sax
		Bari Sax	Tenor Sax
			Bari Sax
Piano	Piano	Piano	Piano
Bass	Bass	Bass	Bass
Guitar	Guitar	Guitar	Guitar
Drums	Drums	Drums	Drums

FIG. 22.21. Four Ensembles for Arranging Practice

NOTES

LESSON 23

Open Voicing

Thus far, the only form of open voicing discussed has been that produced by dropping the second voice of a close block harmonization down one octave.

FIG. 23.1. Open Voicing: Dropping Voice 2

Many other forms of open voicing may be effectively used, but for best results, certain factors must be considered and observed.

1. In closed block voicing (and 2nd dropped, usually), the ear tends to identify melody and to accept a concerted harmonization under it without separating the bottom note from the rest of the chord.

2. The lower or more widespread a chord is voiced, the more important it becomes to have a "strong" function (i.e., root or 5) on the bottom.

3. The relative strength and sonority of an open chord is largely determined by the position of the two bottom notes. It is important that you observe the following "low-interval" limits. Do not use voicings where the interval between the two bottom notes lies in a register lower than that indicated.

NOTE: Do not use a high degree as the bottom voice of any open chord.

FIG. 23.2. Low-Interval Limits

FOUR-PART VOICINGS

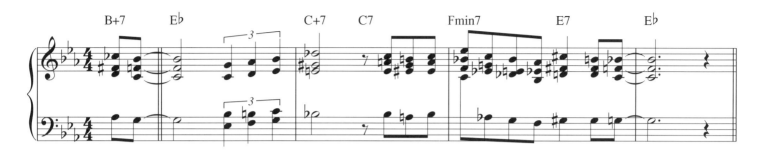

FIG. 23.3. Four-Part Block Harmonization (2nd Voice Dropped 8vb)

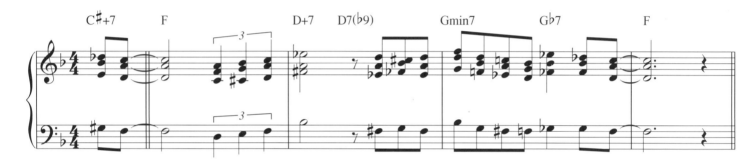

FIG. 23.4. Four-Part Block Harmonization (3rd Voice Dropped 8vb)

FIG. 23.5. Four-Part Block Harmonization (2nd and 4th Voices Dropped 8vb; use in sax section only.)

In actual practice, it is not necessary to adhere to just one of these voicings in harmonizing a melodic line. Any of these open voicings (and closed) may be freely intermingled in order to achieve smooth and interesting inner-voice motion.

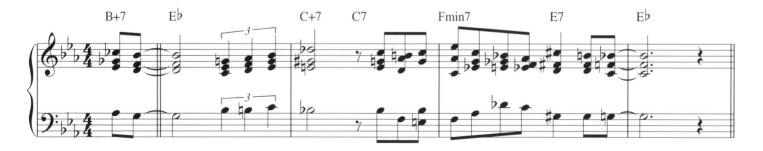

FIG. 23.6. Intermingled Voicing Types

Low–interval limits have been considered in establishing the proper melodic register for each of the preceding examples. Normally, the melody must be transposed from a third to a fifth higher when using 3rd dropped or 2nd and 4th dropped.

FIVE-PART VOICINGS

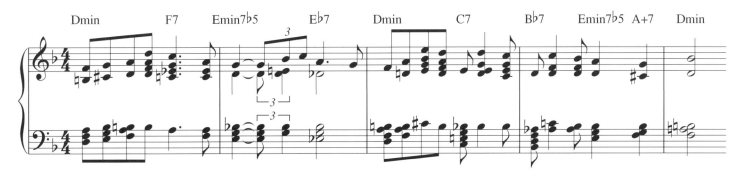

FIG. 23.7. Four-Part Block Harmonization Plus Doubled Lead (2nd Voice Dropped 8vb)

In each of these five-part voicings, where the high degree is in the lead, the related low degree may be substituted for high in place of doubled lead.

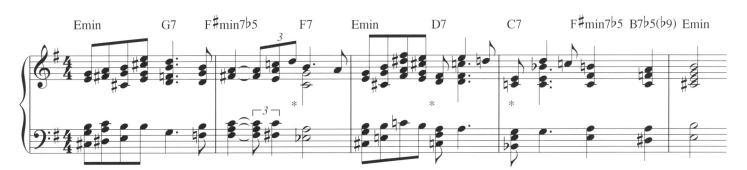

FIG. 23.8. Four-Part Harmonization Plus Doubled Lead (3rd Voice Dropped 8vb). *Not good; see adjustment in figure 23.11 (variable five open voicings)

FIG. 23.9. Four-Part Block Harmonization Plus Doubled Lead (2nd and 4th Voices Dropped 8vb). *Not good; see adjustment in figure 23.11

This technique is especially effective in establishing a strong spread voicing for sustained chords.

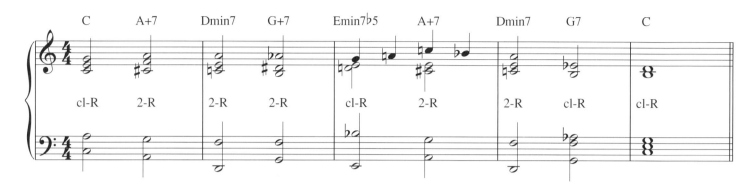

FIG. 23.10. Four-Part Block Harmonization Plus Added Root (Close – 2nd Dropped 8vb – 3rd Dropped 8vb)

Again, any of these five open voicings (and closed) may be intermingled in harmonizing a melodic line. Wherever possible, try to establish root or 5 on the bottom of any sustained chord.

FIG. 23.11. Intermingled Voicing Types

A careful study of the following examples will help in developing an understanding of variable five-part open voicing. When working with open voicings, try to remember the following general principles in addition to those given at the beginning of this lesson:

1. Closed or semi-open voicings are most effective in harmonizing fast moving passages.

2. Widespread voicings, with root on the bottom, are most effective on notes of relatively long duration and in sustained passages.

3. Use variable open voicings primarily to achieve smooth and interesting inner-voice motion and to establish a strong bottom voice on notes of long duration.

4. Normally, widespread voicings are more effective in saxes than in brass.

Voicing Example 4

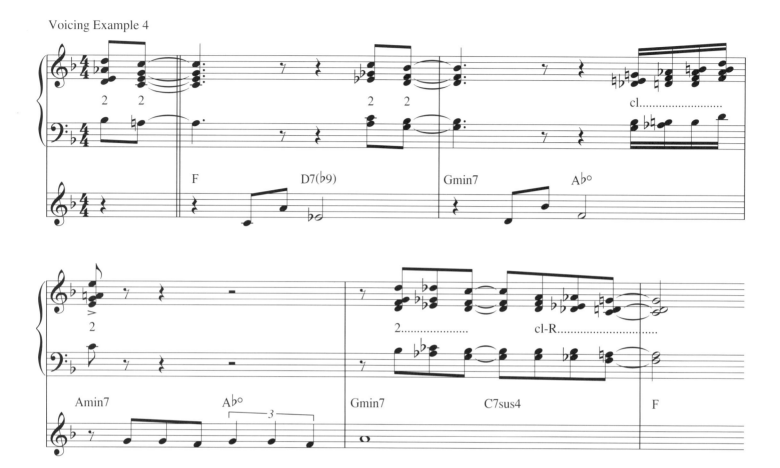

FIG. 23.12. Wide Voicings for Sax Section

ASSIGNMENT

1. Harmonize each of the following melodies for a four-sax section (ATTB) using:

    a. Closed position

    b. 2nd voice dropped 8vb

    c. 3rd voice dropped 8vb

    d. 2nd and 4th voices dropped 8vb

    e. any combination of the above

If considered advisable, melody may be transposed to a different key before completing the harmonization.

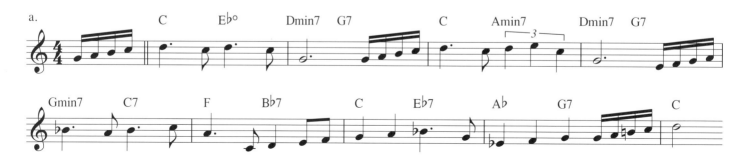

FIG. 23.13. Transposing the Melody for Harmonization

2. Compose a background to each of the following given melodies in each case, and indicate the instrumentation you are picturing for the solo and for the background. Use any of the voicings listed in problem 1. The given melody may be altered or transposed before harmonizing.

FIG. 23.14. Practice Melodies

3. Harmonize each of the following melodies for a five-part sax section using:

   a. Closed position: doubled lead

   b. 2nd voice dropped 8vb: doubled lead

   c. 3rd voice dropped 8vb: doubled lead

   d. 2nd and 4th voices dropped 8vb: doubled lead

   e. closed position: added root

   f. 2nd voice dropped 8vb: added root

   g. 3rd voice dropped 8vb: added root

   h. any combination of the above

Again, the original melody may be transposed or altered in any way.

FIG. 23.15. Practice Melodies

4. Compose a background to each of the following melodies using any of the voicings indicated in problem 3. In each case, indicate instrumentation for which you are writing.

FIG. 23.16. Practice Melodies

The given chord changes to each of the melodies in the assignment may be reharmonized wherever you feel that other chords would be more effective with the particular voicings you are using.

5. Score any standard tune of your choice as follows:

> Trumpet Solo
>
> Five-Part Sax Background (open position)
>
> Bass
>
> Drums
>
> Guitar
>
> Piano

6. Score any standard tune of your choice as follows:

> Five-Part Sax Soli (open position)
>
> Bass
>
> Drums
>
> Guitar
>
> Piano

Larger Ensemble Voicings

FIVE SAXES

Although the subject of soli voicings for a five-sax section has been covered in preceding lessons, there are some other techniques that may often be effectively used.

Free Lead

In a *free lead* voicing, the lead alto moves freely while the other four voices (A, T, T, B) provide a sustained or semi-sustained background. Free lead is often intermingled with conventional five-part soli voicing.

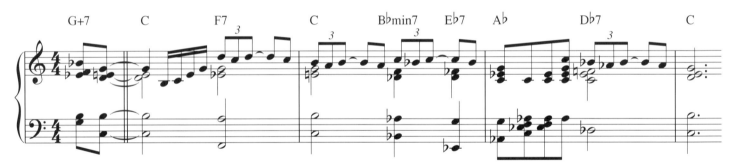

FIG. 24.1. Free Lead Voicings

"Pastels" Voicing

The name "pastels voicing" is taken from the Stan Kenton arrangement of "Opus in Pastels," which utilizes this style of sax-section writing. The two altos play a duet style soli (preferably in thirds) while the three lower voices (T, T, B) provide a strong sustained background. Most effective voicings for the three lower saxes are illustrated in the following chart:

Tenor	3	3	7
Tenor	5	7	3
Bari.	1	1	5

FIG. 24.2. Effective Voicings for Lower Saxes

Use high degrees freely in writing the alto duet and, again, remember that this style of writing may be effectively intermingled with conventional sax-soli voicing. Following is an example of "pastels" voicing for a five-part sax section.

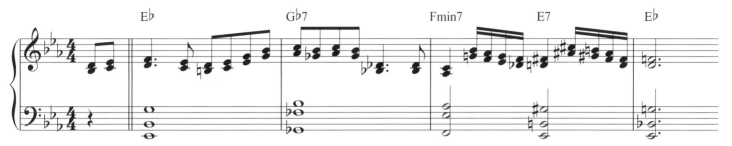

FIG. 24.3. "Pastels" Voicing

Free Baritone

Free baritone voicing consists of a four-part sax soli (A, A, T, T) in closed, 2nd dropped, 3rd dropped, or variable open position with an independent baritone sax part. Since it will, for the most part, constitute a sustained line, the bari part should use root or 5 when it attacks with the rest of the section. Where the upper four voices sustain, the baritone part may fill in the connecting melodic motion.

FIG. 24.4. Free Baritone Voicing

All of the sax voicings discussed in previous lessons may be intermingled with the three special cases described in this lesson, in composing a sax soli.

FIG. 24.5. Intermingled Voicing Types

SIX BRASS

When there are six instruments in a brass section, it will usually be three trumpets
and three trombones.

1. Lead and voice 2 doubled

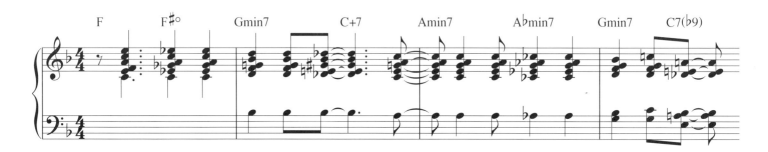

FIG. 24.6. Lead and Voice 2 Doubled

2. Lead and voice 3 doubled

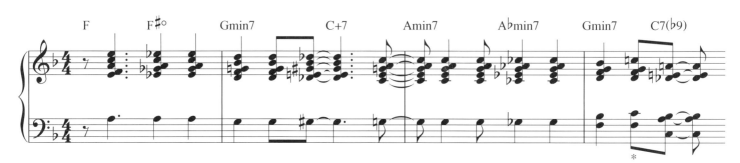

* Substitute low for high in
place of doubled lead.

FIG. 24.7. Lead and Voice 3 Doubled

3. Lead and voice 3 doubled, voice 2 dropped 8vb

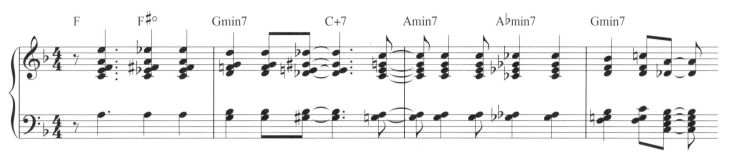

FIG. 24.8. Lead and Voice 3 Doubled, Voice 2 Dropped 8vb

4. Lead and voice 4 doubled, voice 2 dropped 8vb

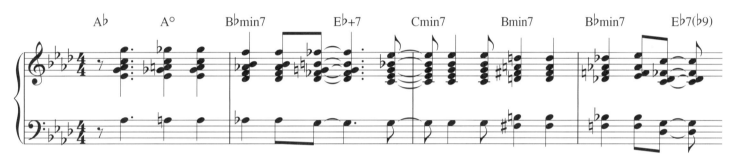

FIG. 24.9. Lead and Voice 4 Doubled, Voice 2 Dropped 8vb

5. Lead and voice 2 doubled, voice 3 dropped 8vb

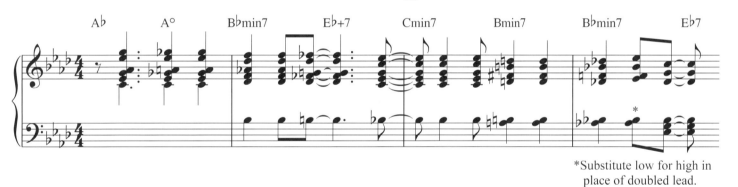

*Substitute low for high in
place of doubled lead.

FIG. 24.10. Lead and Voice 2 Doubled, Voice 3 Dropped 8vb

It is possible to intermingle any of these five brass voicings to assure strong voicing on open sustained chords or to avoid violating low-interval limits as outlined in lesson 23.

SEVEN BRASS

A brass section with seven members typically includes four trumpets and three trombones.

    1.   Lead, voice 2, voice 3 doubled

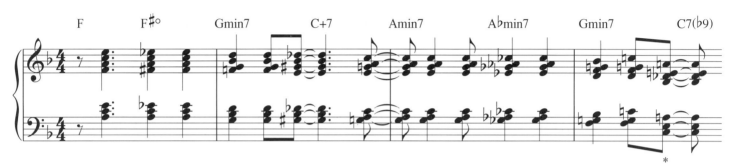

*Substitute low for high to
avoid ♭9 on bottom.

FIG. 24.11. Lead, Voice 2, Voice 3 Doubled

    2.   Trombones: basic chord sound (1-3-5, 1-3-6, 1-3-7, 3-5-7)

        Trumpets: four-part block (closed, dropped 2, or dropped 3)

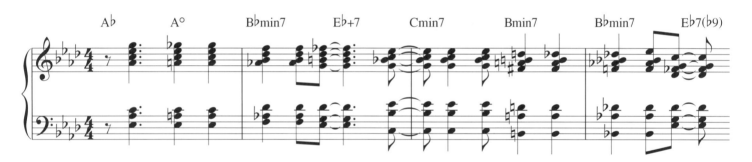

FIG. 24.12. Trombones: Basic Chord, Trumpets: Four-Part Block Voicing

    3.   Trombones: basic chord sound

        Trumpets: separate four-part upper structure (usually triads) with trumpet
4 doubling the lead one octave lower.

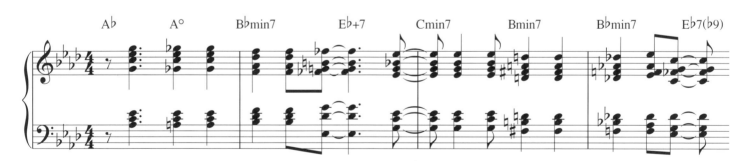

FIG. 24.13. Trombones: Basic Chord, Trumpets: Separate Four-Part Upper Structure with
Doubled Lead

CONCERTED VOICINGS

A *concerted voicing* includes both brass and saxophones.

The expression "soli" is used to indicate a passage scored for one section; the term "tutti" indicates a passage played by the entire ensemble (in the case of the dance-based, brass plus saxes).

There are virtually unlimited possibilities for combining the two sections, and it would be impossible to catalogue them all. Following are examples of those "tutti" voicings that are most commonly used and have generally proven to be effective. Range, low-interval limits, and general quality of sound desired should all be determining factors in deciding which to use.

NOTE: To simplify analysis of the following examples, four brass and four saxes have been used.

    1.   Saxes built down from voice 2 of brass.

*Lead alto doubles 2nd trumpet throughout.

FIG. 24.14. Saxes Built Down from Brass Voice 2

    2.   Saxes built down from voice 3 of brass.

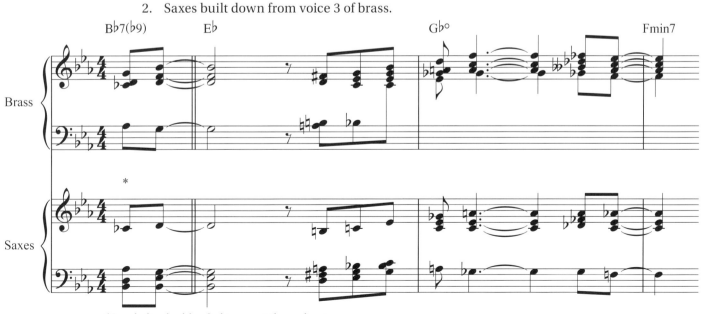

*Lead alto doubles 3rd trumpet throughout.

FIG. 24.15. Saxes Built Down from Brass Voice 3

3.   Saxes built down from voice 4 of brass.

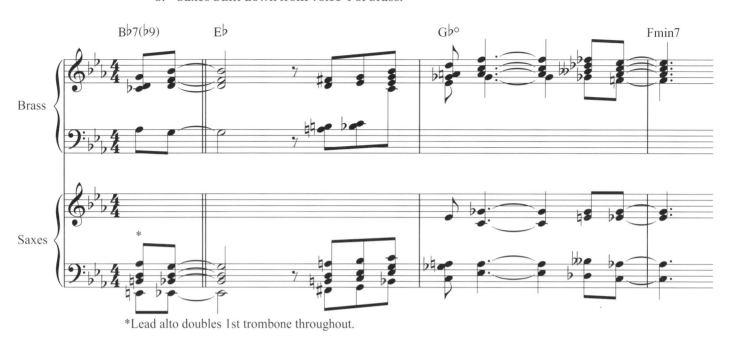

*Lead alto doubles 1st trombone throughout.

FIG. 24.16. Saxes Built Down from Brass Voice 4

4.   Non-constant lead line composed for lead alto before harmonizing rest of sax section.

FIG. 24.17. Non-Constant Lead Line

It is important that you understand that these examples illustrate only a very few of the many, many possibilities for concerted voicing. For purposes of illustration variable open voicing has been used freely, but it is, of course, possible to use constant closed, voice 2 dropped, etc. Mechanical couplings and mechanical open voicings are effective and will usually result in a good ensemble sound in upper, middle, and medium-low registers.

BRASS SOLI WITH HARMONIZED SAX BACKGROUND

To complete our discussion of ensemble voicings, it is also possible to have a brass soli with a harmonized sax background; or a sax soli with a harmonized brass background. All principles of background writing as covered earlier in the course still apply. Simply harmonize both sections.

FIG. 24.18. Brass Soli with Harmonized Sax Background

ASSIGNMENT

1. (a) Score melody a for five saxes using "free lead."

   (b) Score melody b for five saxes using "pastels voicing."

   (c) Score melody c for five saxes using "free bari."

a.

b.

c.

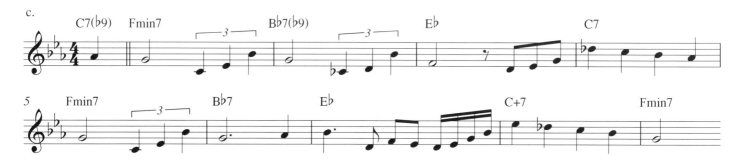

FIG. 24.19. Practice Melodies

2. Score any standard tune of your choice for five saxes, intermingling the three styles described in this lesson with conventional sax voicing.

3. Harmonize the following melody for six brass. Transpose the original melody to a key you consider suitable. Close, open, or variable voicing may be used.

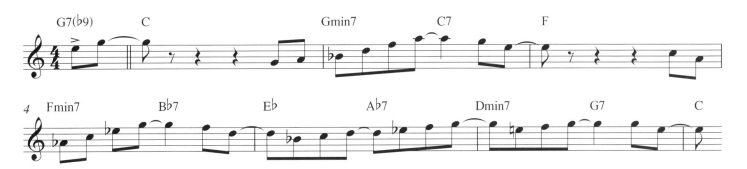

FIG. 24.20. Practice Melody

4. Harmonize the following melody for seven brass. Transpose the original melody to a key you consider suitable. Closed, open, or variable voicing may be used.

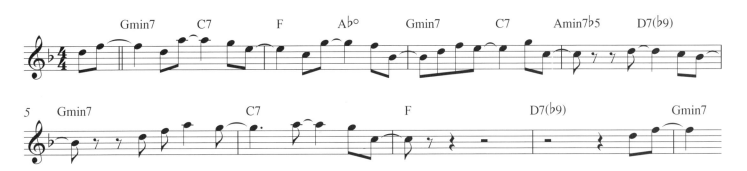

FIG. 24.21. Practice Melody

5. Score any standard tune of your choice for six brass, five saxes, and rhythm section, using concerted ensemble voicings.

6. Score any standard tune of your choice for seven brass, five saxes, and rhythm section as follows:

1st 8 bars	–	brass soli
2nd 8 bars	–	brass soli, sax background
3rd 8 bars	–	brass background, sax soli
4th 8 bars	–	concerted ensemble

Planning and Constructing an Arrangement

PLANNING

The primary objective in planning an arrangement is to produce a musical work that has logical and sensible continuity from beginning to end. You must keep in mind that the listener will hear the arrangement as a unified whole and not as a series of isolated sections.

After selecting the tune to be arranged and the instrumentation (or after these are selected for you by the requirements of a specific arranging assignment), do not start the actual scoring until you have done the following:

1. Determine the overall length of the arrangement (one and one-half choruses, two choruses, etc.).

2. Decide which soloists or sections are to be featured.

3. Consider the style of the band for which you are writing and the adaptability of the tune of this style.

4. Work out a set of chord changes that you feel are basically correct and suitable (although these changes may be reharmonized during the course of the arrangement).

5. Familiarize yourself thoroughly with the tune and the chord changes, and if possible, simply think about the arrangement for a while.

Once you have sat down with score pad and pencil (and eraser), the entire arrangement should be sketched from beginning to end. Sketching simply consists of filling in section lead lines without bothering to complete the harmonization. By doing this at one sitting, you will be able to picture the arrangement as a complete unit with all phrases visualized at the same tempo and with the same feeling. Disregarding this procedure may often result in a series of excellent eight-bar phrases that never seem to sound quite right when played in succession.

The exception to this is the composing of the introduction. If it is not a thematic introduction, it is often advisable to wait until the rest of the arrangement is scored so that some rhythmic, melodic, or harmonic idea that is related to the arrangement itself can be utilized.

FORM

Form, meaning the "logical overall construction and sensible relationship between adjacent sections," is what we are concerned with rather than form meaning "the adherence to formal restrictions and planning." Again, if the arrangement is conceived as a whole and, assuming that personal musical taste based on experience and association is adequate, good "form" should automatically result.

PLANNING TIME DURATION

"Clock-time" duration is an important factor in planning any arrangement. The average dance-band arrangement ranges between 2:30 minutes/seconds and 3:30 minutes/seconds. If the arrangement is to be recorded, plan on 2:15 minutes/seconds to 3 minutes. These time durations apply primarily to commercial arrangements. Production numbers and jazz arrangements may normally be of any desired length.

The following formula may be used in determining exact clock-time duration.

$$\frac{\text{M.M.}}{60} = \frac{\text{Number of beats}}{\text{Clock-time (in sec.)}}$$

Simply translated, this formula becomes:

$$\frac{\text{Number of beats in a minute (M.M.)}}{\text{Number of seconds in a minute (60)}} = \frac{\text{Number of beats in arrangement}}{\text{Number of seconds in arrangement}}$$

EXAMPLE:

M.M. (metronome marking) = 92

Number of beats (4-bar intro, 1 and ½ choruses; 4/4 time) = 208

Clock-time = x

The formula now appears as:

$$\frac{92}{60} = \frac{208}{x}$$

To solve for "x," simply cross-multiply as follows:

$$92\,x = 60 \times 208$$
$$92\,x = 12{,}480$$
$$x = 12{,}480 \text{ divided by } 92$$
$$x = 135 \text{ seconds (2:15 minutes/seconds)}$$

EXAMPLE:

M.M. (metronome marking) = 112

Number of beats (4-bar intro, 2 choruses, 8-bar tag; 4/4 time) = 304

Clock-time = x

$$\frac{112}{60} = \frac{304}{x}$$

Again, cross-multiply to find "*x:*"

$$112\,x \;=\; 60 \times 304$$

$$112\,x \;=\; 18{,}240$$

$$x \;=\; 18{,}240 \text{ divided by } 112$$

$$x \;=\; 163 \text{ seconds } (2{:}43 \text{ minutes/seconds})$$

This same formula may be used (a) when the clock-time is predetermined and the length of the arrangement is to be computed, or (b) when the clock-time and the length are predetermined and the metronome marking is to be computed.

EXAMPLE:

(a) Clock-time = 204 seconds

M.M. = 80

Number of beats = *x*

$$\frac{80}{60} \;=\; \frac{x}{204}$$

(b) Clock-time = 204 seconds

Number of beats = 272

M.M. = *x*

$$\frac{x}{60} \;=\; \frac{272}{204}$$

SCORING

Throughout the last few lessons of the course, we have used just two staves for the brass section and two staves for the sax section. It is now advisable to start using the method of scoring employed by most professional arrangers. Figure 25.1 (a) and figure 25.1 (b) are exactly the same, the only change being that each instrument is notated on a separate stave in the latter illustration.

NOTE: Many arrangers prefer to write "transposed" scores—i.e., with each instrument already transposed rather than in the concert key.

FIG. 25.1. Concert Score Example

GENERAL SUGGESTIONS

1. Try to establish some identifying characteristic in each arrangement. This may take the form of a melodic or rhythmic motif, or a particular orchestral timbre that recurs during the arrangement.

2. Always be aware of the limitations as well as the capabilities of the instrumentalists who will be performing your arrangement. Take advantage of the strengths and avoid writing passages that are beyond the technique of the individual players.

3. Experiment freely with different tone colors and combinations of instruments (trombone lead over saxes; clarinets, tenors, and cup-muted brass; two trombones, two tenors, bari., etc.).

4. If possible, have everything you write played by the proper instrumentation. This is the only way in which you will be able to relate your ideas to the resulting orchestral sound.

5. Take advantage of reharmonization techniques to provide harmonic interest. It is not necessary to use the same chords each time a melodic phrase is repeated.

6. Do not expect to write fluently and professionally until you have written and heard at least twenty to forty arrangements.

7. Study and analyze the scores of other arrangers. Strongly recommended is the "Jazz in the Classroom" LP and score series issued by Berklee College of Music.

ASSIGNMENT

1. Write a complete arrangement of the following tune (or any other standard tune of your choice) for seven brass, five saxes, and rhythm section.

2. Submit to your instructor any specific questions you may have regarding the techniques covered in this course.

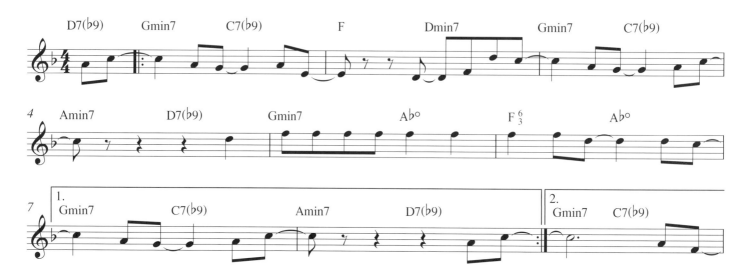

FIG. 25.2. Melody for Problem 1

CODA

The program of study that you have just completed is as all-inclusive and as comprehensive as the length and scope of this course allow. The assignments have been designed to provide you with a practical working knowledge of each technique and the ability to apply these techniques in your playing and arranging.

Your progress from this point on will depend largely on the amount of time you devote to playing, composing, arranging, and listening. It is certainly possible, however, that a good instructor will be able to add to your basic fund of knowledge and make you aware of certain elements of musical taste which may not be a part of your present thinking.

There are also many other aspects of musical study such as composition, cue writing, ear training, instrumental coaching, etc., which will contribute greatly to your general musical knowledge, and you should think of this as one of the intermediate steps rather than as the ending point of your musical education.

Just as soon as your final assignment is submitted and corrected, you will receive a certificate from the Berklee School of Music attesting to the fact that you have successfully completed this program of correspondence study.

Should you have any comments regarding the correspondence course, we would sincerely appreciate hearing of your reaction.

We have enjoyed having the opportunity to work with you and wish you every success in your musical activities.

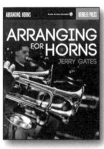

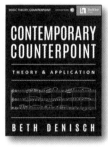

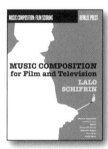

More Fine Publications

GUITAR

BEBOP GUITAR SOLOS
by Michael Kaplan
00121703 Book $16.99

BLUES GUITAR TECHNIQUE
by Michael Williams
50449623 Book/Online Audio...........$24.99

BERKLEE GUITAR CHORD DICTIONARY
by Rick Peckham
50449546 Jazz – Book........................$12.99
50449596 Rock – Book........................$12.99

BERKLEE GUITAR STYLE STUDIES
by Jim Kelly
00200377 Book/Online Media...........$24.99

CLASSICAL TECHNIQUE FOR THE MODERN GUITARIST
by Kim Perlak
00148781 Book/Online Audio..............$19.99

CONTEMPORARY JAZZ GUITAR SOLOS
by Michael Kaplan
00143596 Book.......................................$16.99

CREATIVE CHORDAL HARMONY FOR GUITAR
by Mick Goodrick and Tim Miller
50449613 Book/Online Audio.............$19.99

FUNK/R&B GUITAR
by Thaddeus Hogarth
50449569 Book/Online Audio............$19.99

GUITAR SWEEP PICKING
by Joe Stump
00151223 Book/Online Audio $19.99

INTRODUCTION TO JAZZ GUITAR
by Jane Miller
00125041 Book/Online Audio..............$19.99

JAZZ GUITAR FRETBOARD NAVIGATION
by Mark White
00154107 Book/Online Audio..............$19.99

JAZZ SWING GUITAR
by Jon Wheatley
00139935 Book/Online Audio.............$19.99

METAL GUITAR CHOP SHOP
by Joe Stump
50449601 Book/Online Audio $19.99

A MODERN METHOD FOR GUITAR – VOLUMES 1-3 COMPLETE*
by William Leavitt
00292990 Book/Online Media $49.99
*Individual volumes, media options, and supporting songbooks available.

A MODERN METHOD FOR GUITAR SCALES
by Larry Baione
00199318 Book.......................................$10.99

READING STUDIES FOR GUITAR
by William Leavitt
50449490 Book.......................................$16.99

Berklee Press publications feature material developed at Berklee College of Music. To browse the complete Berklee Press Catalog, go to
www.berkleepress.com

BASS

BERKLEE JAZZ BASS
by Rich Appleman, Whit Browne & Bruce Gertz
50449636 Book/Online Audio...........$19.99

CHORD STUDIES FOR ELECTRIC BASS
by Rich Appleman & Joseph Viola
50449750 Book.......................................$17.99

FINGERSTYLE FUNK BASS LINES
by Joe Santerre
50449542 Book/Online Audio...........$19.99

FUNK BASS FILLS
by Anthony Vitti
50449608 Book/Online Audio...........$19.99

INSTANT BASS
by Danny Morris
50449502 Book/CD.................................$9.99

METAL BASS LINES
by David Marvuglio
00122465 Book/Online Audio.............$19.99

READING CONTEMPORARY ELECTRIC BASS
by Rich Appleman
50449770 Book.......................................$19.99

ROCK BASS LINES
by Joe Santerre
50449478 Book/Online Audio...........$22.99

PIANO/KEYBOARD

BERKLEE JAZZ KEYBOARD HARMONY
by Suzanna Sifter
00138874 Book/Online Audio $24.99

BERKLEE JAZZ PIANO
by Ray Santisi
50448047 Book/Online Audio $19.99

BERKLEE JAZZ STANDARDS FOR SOLO PIANO
arr. Robert Christopherson, Hey Rim Jeon, Ross Ramsay, Tim Ray
00160482 Book/Online Audio $19.99

CHORD-SCALE IMPROVISATION FOR KEYBOARD
by Ross Ramsay
50449597 Book/CD $19.99

CONTEMPORARY PIANO TECHNIQUE
by Stephany Tiernan
50449545 Book/DVD...........................$29.99

HAMMOND ORGAN COMPLETE
by Dave Limina
00237801 Book/Online Audio $24.99

JAZZ PIANO COMPING
by Suzanne Davis
50449614 Book/Online Audio.............$19.99

LATIN JAZZ PIANO IMPROVISATION
by Rebecca Cline
50449649 Book/Online Audio $24.99

PIANO ESSENTIALS
by Ross Ramsay
50448046 Book/Online Audio $24.99

SOLO JAZZ PIANO
by Neil Olmstead
50449641 Book/Online Audio...........$39.99

DRUMS

BEGINNING DJEMBE
by Michael Markus & Joe Galeota
00148210 Book/Online Video..............$16.99

BERKLEE JAZZ DRUMS
by Casey Scheuerell
50449612 Book/Online Audio.............$19.99

DRUM SET WARM-UPS
by Rod Morgenstein
50449465 Book.......................................$12.99

A MANUAL FOR THE MODERN DRUMMER
by Alan Dawson & Don DeMichael
50449560 Book.......................................$14.99

MASTERING THE ART OF BRUSHES
by Jon Hazilla
50449459 Book/Online Audio............$19.99

PHRASING
by Russ Gold
00120209 Book/Online Media $19.99

WORLD JAZZ DRUMMING
by Mark Walker
50449568 Book/CD................................$22.99

BERKLEE PRACTICE METHOD

GET YOUR BAND TOGETHER
With additional volumes for other instruments, plus a teacher's guide.
Bass
by Rich Appleman, John Repucci and the Berklee Faculty
50449427 Book/CD $19.99
Drum Set
by Ron Savage, Casey Scheuerell and the Berklee Faculty
50449429 Book/CD...............................$14.95
Guitar
by Larry Baione and the Berklee Faculty
50449426 Book/CD...............................$19.99
Keyboard
by Russell Hoffmann, Paul Schmeling and the Berklee Faculty
50449428 Book/Online Audio............$14.99

VOICE

BELTING
by Jeannie Gagné
00124984 Book/Online Media..............$19.99

THE CONTEMPORARY SINGER
by Anne Peckham
50449595 Book/Online Audio...........$24.99

JAZZ VOCAL IMPROVISATION
by Mili Bermejo
00159290 Book/Online Audio.............$19.99

TIPS FOR SINGERS
by Carolyn Wilkins
50449557 Book/CD $19.95

VOCAL WORKOUTS FOR THE CONTEMPORARY SINGER
by Anne Peckham
50448044 Book/Online Audio..........$24.99

YOUR SINGING VOICE
by Jeannie Gagné
50449619 Book/Online Audio.............$29.99

WOODWINDS & BRASS

TRUMPET SOUND EFFECTS
by Craig Pederson & Ueli Dörig
00121626 Book/Online Audio.............$14.99

SAXOPHONE SOUND EFFECTS
by Ueli Dörig
50449628 Book/Online Audio...........$15.99

THE TECHNIQUE OF THE FLUTE
by Joseph Viola
00214012 Book.........................$19.99

STRINGS/ROOTS MUSIC

BERKLEE HARP
by Felice Pomeranz
00144263 Book/Online Audio............$19.99

BEYOND BLUEGRASS BANJO
by Dave Hollander and Matt Glaser
50449610 Book/CD................................$19.99

BEYOND BLUEGRASS MANDOLIN
by John McGann and Matt Glaser
50449609 Book/CD $19.99

BLUEGRASS FIDDLE & BEYOND
by Matt Glaser
50449602 Book/CD...............................$19.99

CONTEMPORARY CELLO ETUDES
by Mike Block
00159292 Book/Online Audio............$19.99

EXPLORING CLASSICAL MANDOLIN
by August Watters
00125040 Book/Online Media..........$22.99

THE IRISH CELLO BOOK
by Liz Davis Maxfield
50449652 Book/Online Audio..........$24.99

JAZZ UKULELE
by Abe Lagrimas, Jr.
00121624 Book/Online Audio.............$19.99

WELLNESS

MANAGE YOUR STRESS AND PAIN THROUGH MUSIC
by Dr. Suzanne B. Hanser and
Dr. Susan E. Mandel
50449592 Book/CD $29.99

MUSICIAN'S YOGA
by Mia Olson
50449587 Book $19.99

NEW MUSIC THERAPIST'S HANDBOOK
by Dr. Suzanne B. Hanser
00279325 Book.......................................$29.99

MUSIC PRODUCTION & ENGINEERING

AUDIO MASTERING
by Jonathan Wyner
50449581 Book/CD...............................$29.99

AUDIO POST PRODUCTION
by Mark Cross
50449627 Book $19.99

CREATING COMMERCIAL MUSIC
by Peter Bell
00278535 Book/Online Media...........$19.99

THE SINGER-SONGWRITER'S GUIDE TO RECORDING IN THE HOME STUDIO
by Shane Adams
00148211 Book $16.99

UNDERSTANDING AUDIO
by Daniel M. Thompson
00148197 Book $34.99

MUSIC BUSINESS

CROWDFUNDING FOR MUSICIANS
by Laser Malena-Webber
00285092 Book..$17.99

ENGAGING THE CONCERT AUDIENCE
by David Wallace
00244532 Book/Online Media...........$16.99

HOW TO GET A JOB IN THE MUSIC INDUSTRY
by Keith Hatschek with Breanne Beseda
00130699 Book.......................................$27.99

MAKING MUSIC MAKE MONEY
by Eric Beall
50448009 Book $29.99

MUSIC INDUSTRY FORMS
by Jonathan Feist
00121814 Book $15.99

MUSIC LAW IN THE DIGITAL AGE
by Allen Bargfrede
00148196 Book......................................$19.99

MUSIC MARKETING
by Mike King
50449588 Book $24.99

PROJECT MANAGEMENT FOR MUSICIANS
by Jonathan Feist
50449659 Book......................................$29.99

THE SELF-PROMOTING MUSICIAN
by Peter Spellman
00119607 Book......................................$24.99

CONDUCTING

CONDUCTING MUSIC TODAY
by Bruce Hangen
00237719 Book/Online Media...........$24.99

MUSIC THEORY & EAR TRAINING

BEGINNING EAR TRAINING
by Gilson Schachnik
50449548 Book/Online Audio...........$16.99

BERKLEE CONTEMPORARY MUSIC NOTATION
by Jonathan Feist
00202547 Book $19.99

BERKLEE MUSIC THEORY
by Paul Schmeling
50449615 Book 1/Online Audio........$24.99
50449616 Book 2/Online Audio.......$22.99

CONTEMPORARY COUNTERPOINT
by Beth Denisch
00147050 Book/Online Audio $22.99

MUSIC NOTATION
by Mark McGrain
50449399 Book......................................$24.99
by Matthew Nicholl & Richard Grudzinski
50449540 Book......................................$19.99

REHARMONIZATION TECHNIQUES
by Randy Felts
50449496 Book......................................$29.99

SONGWRITING/COMPOSING

BEGINNING SONGWRITING
by Andrea Stolpe with Jan Stolpe
00138503 Book/Online Audio...........$19.99

COMPLETE GUIDE TO FILM SCORING
by Richard Davis
50449607 Book.....................................$29.99

THE CRAFT OF SONGWRITING
by Scarlet Keys
00159283 Book/Online Audio...........$19.99

CREATIVE STRATEGIES IN FILM SCORING
by Ben Newhouse
00242911 Book/Online Media...........$24.99

JAZZ COMPOSITION
by Ted Pease
50448000 Book/Online Audio $39.99

MELODY IN SONGWRITING
by Jack Perricone
50449419 Book......................................$24.99

MUSIC COMPOSITION FOR FILM AND TELEVISION
by Lalo Schifrin
50449604 Book.................................... $34.99

POPULAR LYRIC WRITING
by Andrea Stolpe
50449553 Book $15.99

THE SONGWRITER'S WORKSHOP
by Jimmy Kachulis
Harmony
50449519 Book/Online Audio $29.99
Melody
50449518 Book/Online Audio $24.99

SONGWRITING: ESSENTIAL GUIDE
by Pat Pattison
Lyric Form and Structure
50481582 Book.......................................$16.99
Rhyming
00124366 Book $17.99

SONGWRITING IN PRACTICE
by Mark Simos
00244545 Book......................................$16.99

SONGWRITING STRATEGIES
by Mark Simos
50449621 Book......................................$24.99

ARRANGING & IMPROVISATION

ARRANGING FOR HORNS
by Jerry Gates
00121625 Book/Online Audio.............$19.99

BERKLEE BOOK OF JAZZ HARMONY
by Joe Mulholland & Tom Hojnacki
00113755 Book/Online Audio $27.50

IMPROVISATION FOR CLASSICAL MUSICIANS
by Eugene Friesen with Wendy M. Friesen
50449637 Book/CD $24.99

MODERN JAZZ VOICINGS
by Ted Pease and Ken Pullig
50449485 Book/Online Audio..........$24.99

AUTOBIOGRAPHY

LEARNING TO LISTEN: THE JAZZ JOURNEY OF GARY BURTON
by Gary Burton
00117798 Book......................................$27.99

NOTES

NOTES